MW01078118

Celluloid Treasures of the Victorian Era

IDENTIFICATION & VALUES

JOAN VAN PATTEN
AND
ELMER &
PEGGY WILLIAMS

COLLECTOR BOOKS

A Division of Schroeder Publishing Co., Inc.

The current values in this book should be used only as a guide. They are not intended to set prices, which vary from one section of the country to another. Auction prices as well as dealer prices vary greatly and are affected by condition as well as demand. Neither the authors nor the publisher assumes responsibility for any losses that might be incurred as a result of consulting this guide.

Searching For A Publisher?

We are always looking for knowledgeable people considered to be experts within their fields. If you feel that there is a real need for a book on your collectible subject and have a large comprehensive collection, contact Collector Books.

Front cover:
Collar and cuff box, 6¾"x6", $325.00 – 400.00.
Oblong photo album, 9½"x11, $500.00 – 600.00.
Toilet and manicure case w/jewel drawer, 13¾"x7¾"x7¾", $475.00 – 525.00.
Shaving set, 5½"x6"x3¼", $250.00 – 300.00.
Toilet and manicure case, 9"x7½"x3", $275.00 – 325.00.

Back cover:
Upright photo album, 8½"x10½", $450.00 – 525.00.
Handkerchief box, 6½"x6½", $100.00 – 150.00.
Smokers' set 8¼"x5¾"x2½", $175.00 – 225.00.

Cover design by Beth Summers
Book design by Beth Ray

COLLECTOR BOOKS
P.O. Box 3009
Paducah, Kentucky 42002-3009

Contents

Acknowledgments

Collector Books is noted for publishing the finest books on antiques and collectibles and we are very happy to be part of that family. We are especially grateful to Billy Schroeder for the opportunity to have this book published. Without his approval, this book would never have been written. Lisa Stroup, our editor, always does a super job on every project she takes on and we want to thank her for her help. We also want to thank all the others at Collector Books who do so much to make these books extra special.

In the beginning we had the ideas, desire, energy, and most of the ingredients to publish a book about celluloid collectibles. What we did not have was enough items to produce a large book encompassing all the wonderful pieces known to exist. We turned to several casual acquaintances who have been quietly collecting celluloid covered items and requested their help.

The help we received was outstanding! The casual acquaintance quickly disappeared when these generous and gracious collectors welcomed us into their homes and permitted us to photograph their beautiful and unusual collections. The items are mixed throughout this book but each and every piece reflects the beauty, the unusual, and the great variety found in each collection.

This book could not have been published without the help and generosity of these very special people. We are confident that all who view the photos in this book would also extend their very special thanks to the owners of these wonderful collections.

Warren and Leslie Brooks are the owners and operators of the 15th and Penn Antique and Art Center in St. Joseph, Missouri. Warren and Leslie began collecting in 1980, and quickly developed an interest in the Victorian era. Their shop is a reflection of the grandeur and beauty of this time period. Everywhere you look you see beautiful ladies, cherubs, and florals depicted on celluloid items, prints, chinaware, flue covers, and jewelry.

Deb Gentile and Jane Sprunger of Cincinnati, Ohio, are dealers/collectors and have been collecting for 15 years. Among their many collections is that of Victorian celluloid covered boxes, albums, autograph books, and many other unusual items. Deb and Jane are also doll collectors and can be located at the summer Atlanta Doll Show. Their primary interest, however, is the Victorian era, especially celluloid covered collectibles.

Randy and Carla Kenley of New Orleans, Louisiana, are dealers/collectors. They can be found at many of the antique shows throughout the eastern part of the country. They always have a good selection of the highest quality Victorian era collectibles. Their collection of celluloid covered pieces is outstanding and includes many unusual items and quality albums and boxes.

Mike and Sherry Miller of Tuscola, Illinois, are well known collectors of Victorian mesh purses and celluloid covered items. Mike and Sherry have been collecting for eight years and their collection of beautiful boxes, albums, and autograph books is one of the top collections in the country. They are members of the Compact Collectors' Club and spend many days traveling to shows throughout the region in search of the very best.

Tom and Bette Sherman of Cincinnati, Ohio, are dealers/collectors with a variety of interests, especially antique advertising, beaded purses, and Victorian items. Their collection of celluloid boxes, albums, and autograph books greatly enhances the beauty of their many Victorian collectibles. Tom and Bette can be located at the Indianapolis advertising shows.

We wish to express our sincere thanks to everyone who helped with this project. Hopefully, we will see this family of collectors grow in the future. Maybe we can even look forward to a second book of these beautiful and unusual collectibles.

Dedication

About the Authors

Elmer and Peggy Williams have been in the antiques and collectibles business for 20 years. Their primary interest is porcelain and Victorian collectibles, especially the celluloid covered collectibles. They have booths in major antiques and collectibles shows in the Southeast and Midwest states.

Elmer and Peggy have written numerous articles for trade/antique papers. They have done extensive travel throughout the United States taking photographs and obtaining information for this book.

Joan Van Patten is the author of eight books published by Collector Books — *The Collector's Encyclopedia of Nippon Porcelain, First through Fifth Series; Nippon Porcelain Price Guide;* and *The Collector's Encyclopedia of Noritake, First and Second Series.* She has written hundreds of trade paper and magazine articles and is a contributor to *Schroeder's Antiques Price Guide.*

Joan has been on the board of the INCC (International Nippon Collectors' Club) since its inception. She served as its first president and was also the co-founder. She edited and published the *Nippon Notebook* and the *INCC Newsletter* for five years, and she has lectured on the subjects of Nippon and Noritake throughout the United States and Canada.

Research of antiques and collectibles and travel are other major interests of the author.

Candles are lit to illuminate dark chambers. Books are written to enlighten the minds and hearts of the readers. And it is our fervent wish that this book fulfills that aspiration.

Introduction

Although the Victorian era historically ended in 1901, its influence was felt for many years after. This book encompasses what we consider to be the golden age of celluloid collectibles, the period of 1885 – 1915.

Queen Victoria came to the throne in 1837, and by 1861 when her husband, Prince Consort Albert died, the British Empire had more than doubled in size. The Victorian era (1837 – 1901) was a time of modesty and self-righteousness not only in Great Britain but in the United States as well. Victoria ruled for 63 years and due to this long reign her name was given to this age.

Today, in the United States there is a nostalgia for anything Victorian, and celluloid collectibles from this time period are in big demand. The Victorian styled photo albums and boxes of all kinds illustrate this period of history. The pictures featured on these items show the ladies of the day dressed in beautiful hats and graceful flowing garments. The gentlemen are dressed in their finest costumes. Many of the scenes depict a gentle romantic period where the gentleman greeted the lady with courtesy and flowers, and couples sat on swings and settees, or walked in a beautiful setting. The influence of several countries can be detected in the figures and scenes, English, French, Dutch, etc.

Children are shown in a calm and relaxed atmosphere, many times playing with the ordinary toys or games of the day. Animals also appeared on many of the boxes and albums in various settings and scenes. Most of the animals shown are native to North America and the scenes included both domestic and wild animals. Birds and beautiful flowers decorated some of the items while others were adorned with leaves and plants including pansies, roses, violets, and sweet peas. The different seasons of the year were also depicted and mistletoe and holly for Christmas items can be found. The celluloid boxes and albums were big sellers during the Christmas holiday season.

Cupid, the god of love in Roman mythology, appears in many variations, again illustrating the gentleness and the quest for romance which was prevalent in the Victorian era. It is not uncommon to find Cupid in molded relief form, in rare instances the animals also appear embossed.

In 1888, George Eastman introduced the Kodak camera which made photographs more readily available. Exchanging photographs with friends and relatives became a popular pastime and this necessitated the purchase of photo albums in which to store them properly. The celluloid albums are often breathtakingly beautiful. Some even contain music boxes, others had their own stand. Although commercial photography had been flourishing since the 1860s the Kodak camera was now within the reach of most households. Most of the photo albums of this period were diecut for standard-sized photographs.

Autographs were also popular with Victorian era people and we find many wonderful autograph books complete with writings from the friends and relatives of the original owners. Postcard albums are unusual but sometimes, they are found intact with postcards from this time period.

The most popular celluloid collectible of this time period besides the photo albums are the boxes.

Boxes could be purchased in all sizes and for a number of uses. There were so-called work boxes (sewing boxes), jewelry cases, combination toilet and manicure cases, shaving sets, smokers' sets, infants' sets, toilet cases, glove and handkerchief boxes, and also boxes for ties. The boxes were made for practical everyday use. The gentleman could store his finest removable collars and cuffs in the collar and cuff box. In some instances the collars and cuffs

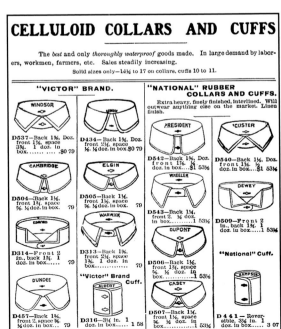

were actually covered with celluloid to protect them from moisture and to lessen the need for washing. This was a real asset when the gentleman was traveling. One patent (#388,287) by Emil Kipper allowed for the collar or cuff to be reversed when occasion demanded.

The old ads state that many of the celluloid items had lithographed pictures, colored chromo centers, or chromo pictures. Others said colored pictures under celluloid. Lithography literally means "to draw on stone." Lithography was invented in 1798 by Aloys Senefelder in Germany. It's an inexpensive means of reproducing art work. A print is made by transferring to paper an inked image drawn on a stone or metal plate. By about the 1830s colored lithographic prints appeared and were known as chromolithographs. During the late 1800s many famous painters used color lithographs, notably Currier and Ives. This form of printing continued into the early twentieth century.

Chromos were produced by inking several stones in different shades and when they were printed in the correct order, the result came out in natural-looking hues. Chromos were immensely popular and permitted even the most modest income households to have brightly colored pictures on their walls. It also allowed for them to have copies of famous oil painting on many of their celluloid items.

Old ads describe some of the scenes portrayed — colonial pictures, Asti and Gainsborough heads, Court dames, juvenile scenes, landscape and sweetheart pictures, beautiful women, natural tinted bust figures, woodland maids, flower girls, colonial lads and lasses in bright costumes, Dutch pictures, automobile girls dressed in colored gowns, the list goes on and on.

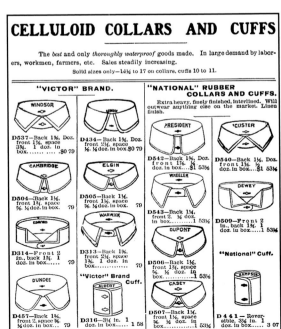

Beautiful trifold mirrors were also produced. Many had brass frames that held the celluloid panels so even when they were closed the mirror was still attractive. Several of these mirrors are patented #387,387, August 7, 1888, which was from a design by Peter Wiederer from Stapleton, New York.

Some of the handles of mirrors, brushes and combs found in the toilet sets were made from a material called gutta-percha. Gutta-percha is a substance resembling rubber. It was obtained from the thick, milky juice of a certain tropical tree found in Malaysia. Gutta-percha is actually an early type of plastic which was patented in the 1850s.

Numerous ads for celluloid items have been found in old catalogs. Butler Brothers was a wholesaler to stores and an ad in their fall 1907 catalog states "Our line is complete, from the low priced popular sellers to the medium and higher priced specialities. Our four houses buy and sell more of these goods than any other concern in the United States."

Many of the old Butler Brothers ads are shown in this book and it can be quite exciting to actually find an ad for an item in one's collection. When comparing today's prices to those in the late 1800s some of the larger toilet cases would cost an equivalent of perhaps $175.00 – 250.00 if they could be purchased new, so they really were quite a luxury. Very few exist today and when they are found they demand a spectacular price.

Collectors should look for items in top condition, the celluloid should not be cracked or peeling. There should not be split seams and hopefully all the hardware will be intact. Quality should be the foremost consideration. One good box or photo album will always be in demand whereas several that are peeling or have pieces of celluloid missing will never be that special. Most collectors feel that the interior condition is generally not as critical as the exterior. Some collectors like portraits best, others prefer scenes or florals. But whatever the design, if you love the item, if it "speaks" to you, it's in good condition, and you can afford it, add it to your collection.

The History of Celluloid

Just what is celluloid and when was it invented? The word celluloid is created from cellulose combined with the Greek suffix oid which means resembling, akin, or like. Celluloid is often used as a generic term for all early plastics and with the advent of celluloid and plastics, life has changed dramatically. It was possible to produce celluloid at a low cost and this product was widely used until it was replaced by synthetics.

Celluloid is composed of cellulose nitrate and camphor, and John Wesley Hyatt, the inventor, has been called "the father of the plastics industry" by many people. His patent #88,634 dated April 6, 1869, was for an improved molding composition to imitate ivory and other substances. The patent states that it will serve as a good substitute for ivory in the manufacture of billiard balls. It was his desire to obtain toughness, hardness, and elasticity in this product. "Take any kind of fibrous vegetable, animal, or even mineral matter, such, for instance, as paper, leather-chips, or asbestos, and reduce the same to a very fine state, so that the fibers can be intimately and thoroughly mixed with a pulverized substance." Hyatt also used gum-shellac, or any other solid, fusible, and adhesive gum or substance, which could be found to answer the required purpose, and reduced the same to a very fine powder. He then thoroughly intermixed this with the fibrous substance, both being in as dry a state as possible. Heat and pressure were applied. The heat was designed to fuse the shellac or other cementing substance used in the compound and cause it to cement the small fibers firmly together to form a solid homogeneous body. Pressure was applied simultaneously with the heat and was designed to compress and pack together the fibers throughout the mass, and thus produce a very dense body. The patent states that the heat simply liberated and softened the shellac sufficiently to make it serve as a cementing agent upon nearly every particle of matter composing the compound.

John W. Hyatt was born in Starkey, New York, in 1837. He was a pressman in a small printing shop in Albany, New York, and fond of an occasional game of billiards. He had no formal chemical training but when he read a Phelan and Collander (the largest supplier of billiards equipment in the U.S.) poster in 1863 offering a prize for $10,000 in gold for billiard balls not made of ivory he started experimenting. Several years later he thought he'd found the right formula.

Elephant tusks had been used to make billiard balls, piano keys, combs, knives, umbrella handles, button hooks, and brushes, etc. for many years and so many elephants had been slaughtered that game preservation laws were passed to end the killing of elephants in Africa. It was feared that these animals would soon be extinct. This caused a shortage of ivory and the hunt was on for a substitute. Although celluloid was never successfully used for billiard balls (it was highly flammable and too brittle), it was used for many other purposes. Celluloid became a substitute for horn, ivory, and tortoise shell in other products, especially combs.

John Hyatt was issued over 200 patents during his lifetime, which is a feat matched by very few other inventors.

Although United States experts credit Hyatt with the patent of celluloid there were several predecessors who also experimented with similar ingredients. Alexander Parkes is considered by some, especially those in Great Britain, to be the founder of the plastics industry. At the 1862 Great International Exhibition in England he showed his new invention of Parkesine. It was a mixture of chloroform and castor oil and he was awarded a bronze medal for excellence of quality. Of course, Parkesine was derived from its inventor's name.

But even before Parkes, in 1846, Schonbein, a chemist in Basle, Switzerland, was dabbling along these same lines. He was distilling nitric and sulfuric acids when he knocked over a container of his experiment. He used a cotton cloth to wipe up the corrosive liquid. The combination of the distilled nitric and sulfuric acids and the cotton cloth became what was commonly known as guncotton, a replacement for gun powder (cotton is one of the purest natural forms of cellulose on earth). This was not the first experiment with nitro-cellulose, however, it was the first time sulfuric acid was used in the mixture. When the news of a replacement for gunpowder reached other countries a panic erupted. England, Russia, France, Austria, and Germany all set up commissions of experts seeking a way to duplicate Schonbein's invention.

During this same time period an apprentice chemist at the College DeFrance made an amazing discovery. Louis Menard (a self-styled artist and "revolutionary poet") was working on a project which was an attempt to duplicate Schonbein's guncotton. He created a new substance he called collodion. Menard discovered that a certain mixture of solvents, ether, and alcohol, would liquefy nitrated cellulose into a smooth clear gelatinous material which he said was in a "colloided" state. When exposed to air, the colloided cellulose nitrate dried into a tough, clear, transparent film. Menard visualized the collodion being used as a varnish, a lacquer, a water-proof coating for cloth, or a moldable solid. Since Menard's interest was in the artistic field he lost interest in collodion when it proved unusable as a lacquer capable of preserving paint.

In 1848 J. Parker Maynard found the first useful application for Menard's collodion. He published an article in the *Boston Medical and Surgical Journal* stating how collodion could be spread over an open wound forming an airtight, watertight, nontoxic seal allowing the skin underneath to heal. Around the same time, Alexander Parkes became intrigued by collodion and began experimenting with it during the years between 1847 and 1862. Parkes visualized producing the collodion in great quantities by mass production to be used in competition with rubber and gutta-purcha products. Unfortunately the solvents used to prepare collodion were far too expensive for mass production and Parkes began mixing his nitrated cellulose with a variety of vegetable oils.

Henry Parkes, Alexander Parkes's brother, patented a system of ornamentation in 1861 which allowed Parkesine to be used as the perfect imitation of tortoise shell, woods, and a variety of other effects.

Alexander Parkes's new material Parkesine was hard as ivory, transparent or opaque. It could also be made flexible and was waterproof. It could be made in the most brilliant colors and used in the solid, plastic, or fluid state. It could be worked in dies and under pressure and cast or used as a coating.

In an effort to reduce his manufacturing cost Parkes began changing his formula resulting in poor quality products which forced the Parkesine Company into receivership. The stage was now set for the plastic revolution.

Between the years of 1864 and 1866 Daniel Spill used the Parkesine formula and manufactured items from it. He disputed Hyatt's patent of 1869 and fought him in court for many years. Other contemporaries were also working along the same lines, W. H. Pierson and G. W. Ray.

A review of old patents indicate that the actual word celluloid was not used until 1872. Hyatt then referred to it in patent #133,229 and it was also listed in the new company name, Celluloid Manufacturing Co. Research indicates that many companies made articles of celluloid but the northeastern portion of the United States seems to have been a hot bed of activity in the celluloid field. There were also companies in England, Germany, Italy, and France.

It is believed that the majority of the boxes and albums were manufactured in the United States but some of the old ads do mention that a few of the items were imported. Alfred Hafely of New York has the only patents (1892) that could be found for boxes, covers for books, and similar articles. He also invented a method for veneering with celluloid covers and corners of books, boxes, etc. (1898). Because these patents are of utmost importance to collectors they have been included in their entirety in this book.

Companies known to manufacture celluloid items

Celluloid Manufacturing Co., Albany, New York, and Newark, New Jersey
Celluloid Novelty Co.
Celluloid Fancy Goods Co.
American Xylonite Co., N. Adams, Massachusetts
American Celluloid and Chemical Manufacturing Co.
Hyatt Manufacturing Co., Albany, New York
British Xylonite Co.
Homerton Manufacturing Co.
Compagnie Francasie du Celluloide
Daniel Spill and Company
Lenel, Bensinger Co.
Celluloid-Fabrik
Celluloid-Fabrik Speyer
Rheinische Sprengstaff Fabrik
Westphalische Anhaltische
Arlington Manufacturing Co.
Mazzuccehelli
Merchants Manufacturing Co.
Fiberloid Company, Indian Orchard, and Newburyport, Massachusetts
Viscoloid Corporation, Leominster, Massachusetts
Lenel Bensinger Co., Mannheim, Germany
Rheinische Gummi-Celluloid Fabrik
S.O. & C., Co., Ansonia, Connecticut

Joseph Wilcox, Inc., Athol, Massachusetts
Sillcocks-Miller Company, So. Orange, New Jersey
Albany Dental Plate Co., Albany, New York
Koch Sons & Co., NYC, New York
Pantasote Leather Co., Passaic, New Jersey
Celluloid Co., New York, New York, and Newark, New Jersey
Rubber and Celluloid Harness Trimming Co., Newark, New Jersey
Self-Developing Plate Co., Ltd., Holborn, England
Whitehead and Hoag, Newark, New Jersey
American Artworks, Cochocton, Ohio
St. Louis Button Co., St. Louis, Missouri
Bastian Brothers, Rochester, New York
Donaldson Brothers, Five Points, New York
Pacific Novelty Co.
Newtown & Merriman
Parisian Novelty Co., Chicago, Illinois
Cruver Mfg. Co., Chicago, Illinois
B. Neuberger
McLoughlin Bros.
E. F. Pulver Co., Rochester, New York
American Art Works, Cushocton

Plant of the Viscoloid Company. Inc., Leominster, Massachusetts, 1901
62 buildings on 40 acres.

Below is a list of some of the known celluloid items manufactured between the years of 1885 and 1915.

Baby rattles
Hair comb ornaments
Combs
Collars and cuffs
Collar buttons
All kinds of boxes
Photo albums
Celluloid handles for
    brushes, nail files, etc.
All types of dressing
    table items
Toys
Prayer books
Autograph albums
Postcard albums
Hairpins
Collar supporters
Billiard balls
Dentures
Pocket mirrors including
    tri-fold purse mirrors
Photo frames
Letter openers
Whisk broom handles
    and holders

Photographic film
Dolls
Table tennis balls
Toothbrushes
Printers' blocks
Nail brushes
Baby brushes
Hat brushes
Boot heels
Dickeys
Jewelry
Shirt bosoms
Dominoes
Medals
Needle cases
Bookmarks
Santa figures
Pin-back buttons
Lap desks
Purses
Dice
Clocks
Desk items
Vases
Button hooks

Tatting shuttles
Sewing tools
Shaving tools
Glove stretchers
Game counters
Shoe horns
Match safes
Pin holders
Stamp cases
Measuring tape cases
Balls
Figurines
Cigarette holders
Games
Pens
Buttons
Spectacle frames
Turban coiffure pins
Turban braid buckles
Calendars

Patents

Important Patents

484,006	10/11/1892
22,788	09/19/1893
505,462	09/26/1893
601,214	03/22/1898

(No Model.)

A. C. HAFELY.

METHOD OF MAKING CORNERS, COVERS, AND LIKE PARTS FOR BOOKS, BOXES, AND SIMILAR ARTICLES OF CELLULOID OR KINDRED MATERIAL.

No. 484,006.   Patented Oct. 11, 1892.

Fig: 1.   Fig: 2.   Fig: 3.   Fig: 4.   Fig: 5.   Fig: 6.   Fig: 7.   Fig: 8.   Fig: 9.   Fig: 10.   Fig: 11.   Fig: 12.

WITNESSES:

INVENTOR

Alfred C. Hafely

BY J. M. Knuttson

ATTORNEY

UNITED STATES PATENT OFFICE.

ALFRED C. HAFELY, OF NEW YORK, N. Y.

METHOD OF MAKING CORNERS, COVERS, AND LIKE PARTS FOR BOOKS, BOXES, AND SIMILAR ARTICLES OF CELLULOID OR KINDRED MATERIAL.

SPECIFICATION forming part of Letters Patent No. 484,006, dated October 11, 1892.

Application filed April 27, 1892. Serial No. 430,900. (No model.)

To all whom it may concern:

Be it known that I, ALFRED C. HAFELY, of New York city, New York, have invented certain new and useful Improvements in Covers and Corners for Boxes, Albums, Picture-Frames, and Like Uses, of which the following is a description, reference being had to the accompanying drawings, which form part of this specification.

The object of my invention is to produce covers, corners, and like articles for books, boxes, albums, and other uses, which shall have certain ornamental features not heretofore accomplished, and which may be readily and economically manufactured, may be somewhat elastic, and of shapes which do not tend to injure surrounding objects. Heretofore metal corners have been made and used, but owing to the hardness and stiffness of the metal the shapes which I contemplate cannot be produced and the sharp stiff edges and corners cut into the covers of the books upon which they are used and scratch or bruise the neighboring books or other articles with which they come in contact. Moreover, it is desirable for producing certain effects, to die, tint, or grain the plain or embossed surfaces of the covers and corners, and this is so expensive and so unsatisfactory where metal is used as to almost preclude such ornamentation. I have, however, discovered a new and useful manner of preparing such covers and corners from thin sheet celluloid or other substance rendered plastic by heat, and the finished article can thereby be made to possess features not heretofore possible by any method I am aware of. The elasticity of the celluloid, together with its plasticity, when warm, render it peculiarly adaptable to my invention, and as it may be made transparent, translucent, or tinted and grained, I am enabled by embossing and by the use of suitable coloring and suitable tinted backings beneath it, to obtain a variety of very beautiful effects.

To such ends my invention consists of and is embodied in the method of forming album, box, book, and like corners, and other ornamental parts, and the articles so produced, substantially as hereinafter described, illustrated, and claimed.

In the accompanying drawings, Figures 1 and 2 are front and rear views of a box-cover made in accordance with my invention. Figs. 3 and 4 are sections of the same on line 4 4 of Fig. 1, and show, respectively, the wooden frame or patrix with and without the applied sheet of celluloid. Figs. 5 and 6 are front and rear views of a book-cover. Figs. 7, 8, and 9 show details of its manufacture. Figs. 10 and 11 show details of a manufacture of an album-corner, and Fig. 12 a rear view of the completed article.

In these views like letters of reference indicate like parts.

In making box-covers according to my invention I may employ a wooden frame B, which is shown in cross-section in Fig. 3, and is provided with ornamental moldings, as shown. The celluloid sheet, cut to the proper size and embossed with ornamental figures, as will hereinafter be described, or plain, if preferred, is then laid upon the frame. A heated matrix corresponding in shape to the frame B is then brought down, and the celluloid, which is heated and rendered plastic thereby, is pressed into shape between the matrix and the frame, the latter forming a patrix therefor, to which the celluloid conforms. It is preferable to first coat the celluloid with celluloid cement, so that the celluloid when pressed into place by the heated die may be firmly cemented to the frame. After this operation the edges of the celluloid sheet project perpendicularly from the frame. They may then be heated and turned down, as in Fig. 2, and a flat heated iron applied to them. By a pressure from or against the heated iron the overlapping corners are thoroughly blended and united. If desired, the corners may be first covered with celluloid cement, so that they may be more readily blended or cemented together. By this means it will be seen a box-cover is produced containing a stiff frame, as shown in Figs. 1 to 4. I form covers for books and albums in a similar manner. Preferably, however, the cover is embossed and its edges turned up at right angles, as shown in Fig. 7, by means of two heated dies which render the material plastic and capable of taking up the curbed outline required. A pad made of wadding or other soft material is then substituted in place of the patrix die, as in Fig.

8, and the corners turned over and secured at the rear of the cover, as shown in Fig. 6, in a manner substantially the same as in the case of the box-cover just described. In this way a soft padded cover—such as is shown in Figs. 5 and 9—may be produced. Leather, basketwork, and other designs may be made use of in forming such a cover and the elasticity and smoothness of the finished surface render it peculiarly adapted for albums and like ornamental uses. The construction may be modified somewhat by substituting a permanent patrix in the process of embossing and turning up the edges upon the back of such patrix to form a cover for either boxes or albums. This is a mere variation of Fig. 1.

In the forms heretofore described the finished article has contained a frame or permanent padding, to which the celluloid covering is secured. In Figs. 10, 11, and 12 is shown, on the other hand, a corner adapted to be fitted over and to be secured to the finished cover of a book or album. In forming this corner the sheet of celluloid is first cut to a suitable blank, as in Fig. 10. This blank has the side flaps c, which turn over the edges of the book, and the flap or tongue d to cover the corner where the two flaps meet. The blank is first pressed between two suitable dies which are heated and render the blank soft and plastic. By these dies the central or exposed portion is embossed with ornamental designs and given the rounded form shown in Fig. 12 at c. The flaps c are turned at right angles on the line F and present the appearance indicated by dotted lines in Fig. 12. The flaps and tongue are then treated with suitable cement and subjected to pressure between the flap back of the patrix and a heated plate. By this action of heat and pressure are secured together and thoroughly blended, as shown in Fig. 11. The corner is now complete and may be removed from the die and the patrix slipped out of it. A full celluloid side or cover of a book may be made in a manner similar to the corner just described, it being only necessary to use a blank, dies, &c., provided with two instead of one corner. The material of which like corners and covers are made may be entirely opaque, translucent, or transparent, or may be in part opaque and in part otherwise. Color effects may be produced by applying color-padding at the back of translucent celluloid or by applying paint or pigment to the under surface. The exposed surface may be ornamented by applying designs of various colors to its embossed surface, and the final polishing by partially removing the colors from the points most in

relief produces an effect of shades and tints which is exceedingly beautiful.

It must not be understood that my invention is limited to the use of celluloid. On the contrary, kindred preparations of cellulose and like substances may be employed and a variety of effects thereby produced.

I am aware that sheet celluloid has been applied to molding by means of heat, vacuum, and external fluid pressure. My method and the articles produced by it are substantially different, both in purpose and in result.

I have now set forth several ways of applying my method and several forms of the article it is intended to produce.

I therefore claim as my own, and desire to secure by these Letters Patent, the following:

1. The method of making covers, corners, and like parts for books, boxes, and other uses of sheet-celluloid or kindred material rendered plastic by heat, which consists of forming up its border by suitable dies first at right angles and then parallel to the cover or corner and uniting them by the application of heat and pressure, substantially as set forth.

2. The method of making covers, corners, and like parts for books, boxes, and other uses of sheet-celluloid or kindred material rendered plastic by heat, which consists of forming up its border by suitable dies first at right angles and then parallel to the cover or corner, uniting and blending them by the application of heat and pressure, and padding or filling the interior so formed, substantially as set forth.

3. The method of making corners, covers, and like parts for books, boxes, and other uses of celluloid or other material that may be rendered plastic by heat, which consists in applying heat and pressure by suitable dies, folding over the borders, and cementing or otherwise securing them together, substantially as set forth.

4. A cover or corner for books, boxes, and like uses, consisting of a sheet of celluloid or kindred material and provided with round corners, the borders of the said cover or corner being folded over upon its back, and a tongue or flap at meeting edges of the said borders, cemented or otherwise secured thereto, substantially as and for the purposes set forth.

In testimony whereof I have hereunto set my hand this 14th day of April, 1892.

ALFRED C. HAFELY.

Witnesses:
FRED. HEMMING,
HAROLD BINNEY.

UNITED STATES PATENT OFFICE.

CHARLES H. FERNALD, OF AYER, MASSACHUSETTS.

DESIGN FOR A CELLULOID SHEET.

SPECIFICATION forming part of Design No. 22,788, dated September 19, 1893.

Application filed August 17, 1893. Serial No. 483,415. Term of patent 7 years.

To all whom it may concern:

Be it known that I, CHARLES H. FERNALD, a citizen of the United States, residing at Ayer, in the county of Middlesex and State of Massachusetts, have invented and produced a new and original Design for a Celluloid Sheet, of which the following is a specification, reference being had to the accompanying drawings, illustrating my design, in which—

Figure 1 is a view of a celluloid sheet having its edge or border made in accordance with my design. Fig. 2 is an edge view of the same. Fig. 3 is an enlarged vertical section of the same.

The leading feature of my design for a celluloid sheet is the border of the same which consists of a fluted edge of peculiar shape lying substantially in the plane of the body of the sheet and presenting a pleasing and attractive appearance.

In the drawings, A designates a sheet of celluloid having a border or edge B fluted substantially in the plane of the body of the sheet in accordance with my design. As shown, the extreme outer edge *c* of the fluted border, which presents a series of curves arranged in serpentine form, is alternately above and below the plane of the body of the sheet, as shown in Figs. 2 and 3, while the inner edge of said fluted border meets or coincides with the plane of the sheet at *d* along its entire length, the appearance of such a sheet when used for a variety of purposes such as booklet covers, cards, ladies' belts, &c., being exceedingly unique and very ornamental and attractive.

What I claim as new, and desire to secure by Letters Patent, is—

The design for a celluloid sheet, substantially as herein shown and described.

Witness my hand this 3d day of July, A. D. 1893.

CHARLES H. FERNALD.

In presence of—
P. E. TESCHEMACHER,
HARRY W. AIKEN.

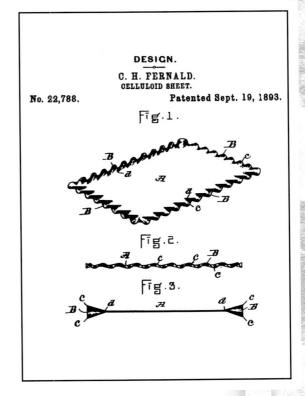

Example of design patent 22,788.

UNITED STATES PATENT OFFICE.

ALFRED C. HAFELY, OF NEW YORK, AND JENS REDLEFSEN, OF BROOKLYN, NEW YORK.

MANUFACTURE OF CELLULOID BOXES.

SPECIFICATION forming part of Letters Patent No. 505,462, dated September 26, 1893.

Application filed November 26, 1892. Serial No. 453,276. (No specimens.)

To all whom it may concern:

Be it known that we, ALFRED C. HAFELY, of New York city, and JENS REDLEFSEN, of Brooklyn, New York, have invented certain new and useful Improvements in the Manufacture of Celluloid-Covered Boxes and Similar Articles, of which the following is a description, reference being had to the accompanying drawings, which form a part of this specification.

Our invention relates particularly to celluloid-covered moldings for the sides of boxes; though generically it will be seen to include many other articles covered with celluloid.

Its object is to cheapen, improve, and simplify the construction of such articles; which we accomplish by the method of procedure, and the product thereof, combined and used substantially as hereinafter described, illustrated, and claimed.

In the accompanying drawings Figures 1 and 2 are face and sectional views of molding made in accordance with our method. Figs. 3 and 4, are like views of a slightly modified construction. Fig. 5 shows our way of utilizing such molding in the manufacture of boxes. Figs. 6, 7, and 8, are views showing the successive steps in the manufacture of a box, and simple apparatus therefor.

In all the figures like letters of reference indicate like parts.

Figs. 1 and 2 show the molding for the sides of a box; Fig. 5, the finished box; and Figs. 6, 7, and 8, the apparatus for and stages of its manufacture, in accordance with the simplest form of our method. In this instance we employ sheet celluloid already embossed and preferably lined on the rear face with paper, muslin, or other fabric for the more ready adhesion of the glue or other cement by which we secure it to the wooden backing. After embossing, the celluloid veneer or facing C is coated with glue or cement. It is then laid, face down, across a heated die D, conforming to the wooden backing as shown. The strip of backing is then placed upon the celluloid as in Fig. 6 and forced into the heated die, turning up the edges of the celluloid and cementing it firmly to the face and edges of the backing. The next step is to turn down the projecting edges of the cellu-

loid, by any suitable hand instrument, onto the back of the wooden strip B, and then to apply pressure from a follower or platen E by placing the whole apparatus (in the position shown in Fig. 7) within a press. Felting or other soft cushion F is placed within the die in order to prevent the obliteration and injury of the embossing. This method of preparing the molding is modified by using plain celluloid and employing a heated embossing die or matrix in place of the felted die just described. In this case the wooden backing also receives the impression, beneath the celluloid, corresponding with the embossing of the celluloid veneer, and for this purpose suitably selected soft wood should be employed.

Figs. 3 and 4 show the celluloid with the paper facing and Figs. 1 and 2 show it without. With the latter it is necessary to use a celluloid solvent as a cement. When the molding is finished it is cut, mitered, and secured together to form a rectangular frame corresponding with the sides of the desired box. The frame so formed is then cut in a plane corresponding to the lines *m—m* of Figs. 2 and 4. Two rectangular frames are thereby produced each having one edge faced with celluloid, as at *c* in the figures, and one edge exposing the severed edge of the wood as at *b* in the figures. One of the frames is employed as the side of the cover of the box and glued by its wooden edge *b* to the wooden face of the box cover or top G. The manufacture of the box tops forms the subject of Patent No. 488,630, issued to A. C. Hafely, December 27, 1892. The top is veneered with celluloid to correspond with the sides, and the veneer extends beneath the lower face of the box top and meets the veneer C but leaves the wood, beyond, bare, for the gluing of the meeting edge *b* of the box sides. The other rectangular frame forms, in corresponding manner, the sides of the lower portion of the box, the bottom being veneered and glued to the sides in the same manner as the top. Figs. 5, and 8, show the finished structure.

Our method of forming and embossing the molding for the boxes may be somewhat modified to enable it to be carried out at a single operation by a simple automatic machine.

As the machine, however, does not form a part of the subject matter of the claims of this present application, but is embodied in the divisional application, Serial No. 477,497, filed by us June 13, 1893, we do not herein set it forth or illustrate it. The sheet celluloid and glued wooden strip are placed together and forced through a guide chute which turns up the edges of the celluloid over the edges of the strip or backing, preparatory to the heating and embossing which may be effected in this case by heated rolls. The projecting edges of the celluloid are turned down upon the rear face of the backing by a second guide chute instead of by hand, and the molding is then run between a second pair of heated rollers subjecting it to a final heat and pressure, which secures the edges upon the back. This, it will be seen, is a mere variation of my method, enabling it to be done more directly and certainly, by means of the machine which carries it out. The details and advantages of this variation will be better understood from the fuller description given in connection with the machine for carrying it out, and it is therefore, unnecessary to go more into detail in this present application.

We have now described our method, our product, and one form of a simple hand apparatus for carrying out our method and making our product, as illustrating one embodiment of our invention.

We have purposely omitted many modifications which are suggested by mere mechanical skill, because to set them forth would obscure rather than to make clear the essential features of our invention.

We therefore claim, desiring to secure by Letters Patent all variations that may be made by mere skill in the art, the following:

1. A box cover, box, or like article, consisting of sides, each faced with celluloid veneer upon its exposed face and one edge, and a top, bottom, or other conjoined part, glued or cemented to the bare edges of the said sides and faced with celluloid veneer extending to and meeting the veneer upon the sides of the said box, but leaving the bare surface of such part in contact with the bare surface of the said side, substantially as, and for the purposes, set forth.

2. A slide for a box or similar article, con-

sisting of a backing B faced with celluloid upon one side and each edge *c* thereof, and divided to form bare edges *b* for securing adjacent parts, and to permit the faced edges *c* to be brought together to form the opposing and meeting edges of the side, substantially as, and for the purposes, set forth.

3. The method of manufacturing sides for celluloid boxes and similar articles, which consists in securing a celluloid facing to the face and edges of the backing by heat and pressure, turning down the projecting edges of the celluloid upon the rear face of the said backing, and then subjecting the whole to heat and pressure in a suitable press, substantially as, and for the purposes, set forth.

4. The method of manufacturing celluloid covered articles which consists in cementing a celluloid facing, conforming and securing it to the backing by heat and pressure, turning down the edges upon the rear face of the backing, and then applying heat and pressure, substantially as and for the purposes set forth.

5. The method of manufacturing sides for celluloid boxes and similar articles, which consists in securing and embossing a celluloid facing upon the face and edges of the backing by suitable cement and by heat and pressure, turning down the projecting edges of the celluloid upon the rear face of the said backing and forcing them firmly into contact with the backing by suitable pressure, substantially as, and for the purposes, set forth.

6. The method of constructing the sides of boxes or similar articles of celluloid, which consists in covering the face and edges of a strip or molding with suitable celluloid veneer, cutting and joining the said molding into a frame corresponding in shape to the form of the finished article of the said article, and then severing the said frame as described, whereby the celluloid-covered edges may be brought together to form the opposing and meeting edges of the said article, substantially as, and for the purposes, set forth.

In testimony whereof we have hereunto set our hands this 7th day of November, 1892.

A. C. HAFELY.
JENS REDLEFSEN.

Witnesses:
MILTON D. F. HOWE,
F. W. GREAVES.

A. C. HAFELY & J. REDLEFSEN.
MANUFACTURE OF CELLULOID BOXES.

No. 505,462. Patented Sept. 26, 1893.

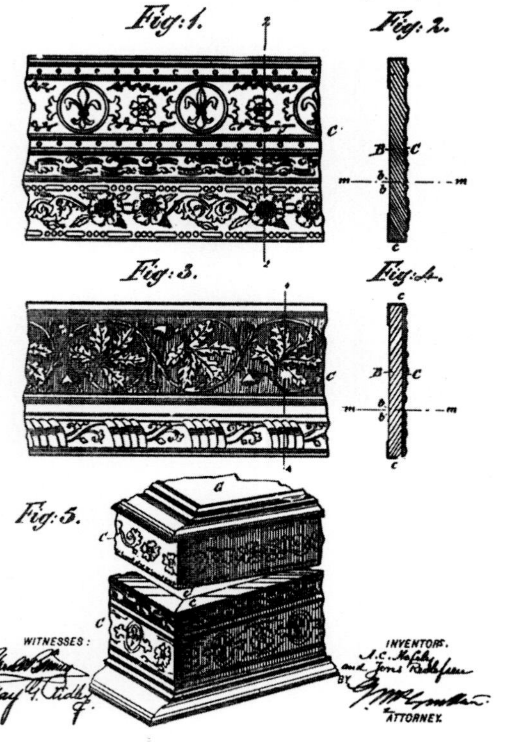

Fig. 1.

Fig. 2.

Fig. 3.

Fig. 4.

Fig. 5.

WITNESSES:

INVENTORS.
A. C. Hafely
and Jens Redlefsen
ATTORNEY.

A. C. HAFELY & J. REDLEFSEN.
MANUFACTURE OF CELLULOID BOXES.

No. 505,462. Patented Sept. 26, 1893.

Fig. 6.

Fig. 7.

Fig. 8.

Witnesses

Inventors
A. C. Hafely and Jens Redlefsen
By their Attorney

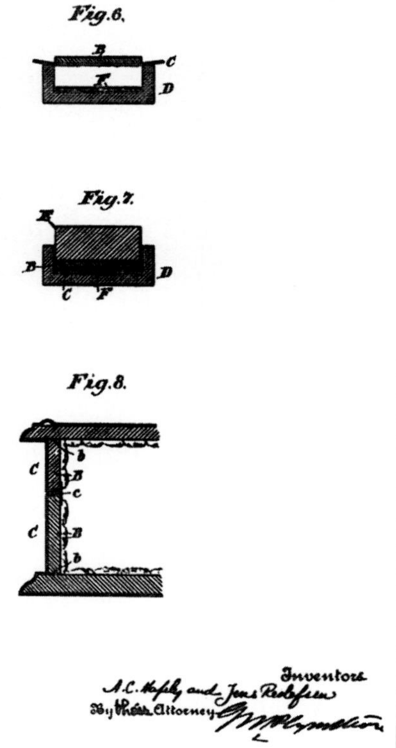

UNITED STATES PATENT OFFICE.

ALFRED C. HAFELY, JENS REDLEFSEN, AND CHARLES A. HAPPE, OF BROOKLYN, NEW YORK.

METHOD OF AND APPARATUS FOR VENEERING WITH CELLULOID COVERS AND CORNERS OF BOOKS, BOXES, &c.

SPECIFICATION forming part of Letters Patent No. 601,214, dated March 22, 1898.

Application filed June 3, 1896. Serial No. 594,120. (No model.)

To all whom it may concern:

Be it known that we, ALFRED C. HAFELY, JENS REDLEFSEN, and CHARLES A. HAPPE, citizens of the United States, residing at Brooklyn, in the county of Kings and State of New York, have invented a new and useful Improvement in Methods of and Apparatus for Veneering with Celluloid the Corners and Covers of Books, Boxes, &c., of which the following is a specification.

Our invention relates to methods and apparatus for veneering with sheet-celluloid or kindred material capable of being rendered plastic by heat the covers and corners for books, boxes, and like uses; and it has for its object to simplify and improve such methods and apparatus and to prevent injury to any embossing and ornamental work that may be upon the sheet-celluloid or kindred material during the process.

It consists of the methods and devices hereinafter more particularly set forth, and claimed in the claims at the end of this specification.

In veneering rounded lids for albums, books, boxes, &c., with sheet-celluloid or similar material capable of being made plastic by heat the main difficulty encountered is to dispose of or prevent the formation of wrinkles or folds in the sheet at the rounded corners of the lid to be veneered or where the surface of the lid rounds together from the straight sides of the lid and rounds down toward the extreme point or the toe of the corner. The words "rounded corners," as employed in this specification, will be used in the said sense of corners rounding down toward the extreme point or toe of the corner as distinguished from corners rounding in a horizontal plane only. At these places where the rounding in the surface of the lid occurs the sheet of celluloid is apt to wrinkle or fold, thus impairing the beauty of the veneered lid and destroying its resemblance to a solid piece of ivory or of such other material as the celluloid is tinted to resemble. Heretofore such wrinkles or folds in the sheet-celluloid have been prevented or disposed of by subjecting the sheet of celluloid or other material to pressure between heated dies of the shape of the cover or corner to be formed, by means of which the sheet has been made, under the influence of the heat and pressure, to permanently conform to the shape of the dies, such a molecular rearrangement of the sheet-celluloid taking place at the corner as to eliminate the folds or wrinkles or to reabsorb them into the sheet. In such a method two dies of the desired shape are required, a male and a female die, the process being substantially one of forming the sheet between the male and female dies under the influence of heat and pressure. The main objection to this method is that the use of the female die is apt to injure the raised, embossed, or ornamental work upon the said sheet, and as such embossed work is used upon nearly all of the sheet-celluloid used for veneering this objection is a serious one. We have discovered a method of successfully veneering such lids with celluloid or kindred material which entirely dispenses with the use of the female die, and which thus avoids all danger of injury to the embossing.

The drawings show the preferred form of our improved apparatus and show apparatus by means of which our improved process can be carried out.

Figure 1 is a vertical section of the same, taken on the line 1 1 of Fig. 2. Fig. 2 is a plan of the same. Fig. 3 is a vertical section taken through the center of a lid which has been veneered, but before the edges of the celluloid sheet have been bent over against the under side of the lid.

A plunger is employed to form the sheet. As shown in the drawings, it consists of an iron block or anvil A of the proper size and shape and a patrix D supported thereon. The patrix D may be integral with the block A, or, as shown in the drawings, it may be a separate piece. In the latter case it may be the lid which is to be veneered.

The patrix D in either case is made in the shape usually employed in lids for album-covers—that is to say, having rounded corners, or corners as above described, which round upward from the horizontal plane of

the under side of the patrix, as shown in Figs. 1 and 3 at *d*. It may also, if desired, have some of its corners rounded in the plane of its under side, as shown at *g g* in Fig. 2. In veneering such a lid or patrix D with celluloid or kindred material the celluloid is apt to form in folds or wrinkles at the corners *d d*, which round upward from the plane of the base of the patrix, and particularly at the corners which also round in a horizontal plane, as at *g g*.

B is an iron ring or gripper surrounding the block or anvil A and following the contour of the anvil. It is mounted upon a series of springs C C, the springs being secured to a circular extension A' of the anvil A. The springs enable the gripper B to work up and down around the anvil A.

E is the sheet of celluloid or kindred material embossed, if it be so desired, with ornamentation at H in the usual manner.

F is an iron ring or clamping-frame, with an opening G in its center corresponding to the shape of the patrix D to be veneered and of the same size.

The operation of the form of our device shown in the drawings is as follows: The patrix D to be veneered is placed upon the plunger A. In the normal position of the gripper B the latter projects slightly above the upper surface of the plunger A, thus holding the patrix D in position. The sheet of celluloid E is then placed over the patrix, as shown in Fig. 1. The clamping-frame F in the form of apparatus shown in the drawings is stationary. The anvil A, with the gripper B, patrix D, and celluloid sheet E, are moved upward by any suitable mechanism until the sheet of celluloid is gripped between the gripper B and the clamping-frame F. The anvil A in its further progress upward forces the celluloid sheet E into the opening G within the clamping-frame F. The gripper B, however, cannot rise any farther, because the clamping-frame F is stationary. The springs C C are accordingly compressed. The patrix D therefore rises into the opening G until its under face is at least up to the level of the upper surface of the ring B. During the operation or before it the metal portions of the apparatus are heated, thus communicating heat to the celluloid sheet. Under the influence of the heat and through the upward movement of the anvil and patrix and the gripping of the celluloid sheet along the edges of the patrix by the gripping devices, gripper B, and clamping-frame F the celluloid sheet is stretched over the patrix D, especially at the rounded corners, and is made to permanently conform to the shape of the patrix, and smooth and slightly-veneered corners are formed without any folding or wrinkling and without destroying in any way the density, elasticity, or polish of the sheet-celluloid. When the patrix is removed from the anvil, it presents the appearance shown in Fig. 3. As the upper surface of the patrix D with the sheet of celluloid on it rises into the opening G of the clamping-frame F the embossing H upon the sheet-celluloid does not come into contact with any female die. It is therefore not in any way affected or injured by the operation. After the patrix D with its veneering-sheet E is taken from the anvil the workman with any suitable tool cuts away the superfluous material of the sheet at the square corners to form a right-angled miter, and at the corners rounded in the plane of the bottom of the patrix D he cuts away the superfluous celluloid, leaving, however, sufficient to form a flap. The the edges of the celluloid on the four straight sides of the patrix are bent over and back on the under side of the patrix. The flap is likewise bent back on the under side of the patrix over or under the adjoining straight sides and the edges of the celluloid sheet are secured to the under surface of the patrix by cement or glue, and the overlapping edges and the flap are secured to one another by pressure and heat or cement in the ordinary manner. The rough edges of the cover at the corners are then sand-papered and the finished celluloid veneer cover is the result.

Various modifications in detail could be made in the process and apparatus without departing from the spirit of our invention. Thus, for instance, if desired, the plunger instead of working from below upward could work from above the sheet downward. The shape of the patrix could be varied or glue or cement might be applied to the under surface of the sheet E before the operation. It is also evident that after the celluloid sheet has been made to conform to the shape of the patrix, as shown in Fig. 3, the patrix D can be removed, if desired, and another and permanent patrix be substituted in its place and the edges of the sheet be turned over onto the back of the second patrix. In this way the first patrix used may be of metal.

What we claim as new, and desire to secure by Letters Patent, is—

1. The method of veneering rounded corners, covers of books, boxes and similar articles, with sheet-celluloid or kindred material capable of being rendered plastic by heat, which consists in gripping the edges of the sheet, applying heat to the sheet and forcing the sheet around the rounded corners of the articles to be veneered, whereby the said sheet will be made to permanently conform to the rounded shape of the corners, substantially as set forth.

2. The method of veneering rounded corners, covers of books, boxes and similar articles, with sheet-celluloid or kindred material capable of being rendered plastic by heat, which consists in gripping the edges of the sheet, applying heat to the sheet and forcing the sheet around the rounded corners of the articles to be veneered, whereby the said sheet will be made to permanently conform to the rounded shape of the corners, and turning

over the projecting edges of the sheet upon the back of the inclosed patrix and securing them thereto, substantially as set forth.

3. The method of veneering rounded corners, covers of books, boxes and similar articles, with sheet-celluloid or kindred material capable of being rendered plastic by heat, which consists in gripping the edges of the sheet, applying heat to the sheet and forcing the sheet around the rounded corners of the articles to be veneered, whereby the said sheet will be made to permanently conform to the rounded shape of the corners, turning over the projecting edges of the sheet upon the back of the inclosed patrix and securing them thereto, and uniting or blending said edges to each other at their overlapping portions, substantially as set forth.

4. The combination with a plunger having its face of the shape of the article to be veneered and adapted to be forced against a sheet of celluloid, of gripping devices to hold the sheet taut, whereby the sheet will be made to permanently conform to the shape of the face of the plunger, substantially as set forth.

5. The combination with a plunger having its face of the shape of the article to be veneered and adapted to be forced against a sheet of celluloid, of a gripper mounted on springs and surrounding the plunger, and a hollow clamping-frame against which the gripper is adapted to press to hold the sheet taut, whereby the sheet, when heated, will be stretched over the face of the plunger within the hollowed-out portions of the clamping-frame, and be made to permanently conform to the shape of the face of the plunger, substantially as set forth.

6. The combination with a plunger having its face of the shape of the article to be veneered and adapted to be forced against a sheet of celluloid, a gripper surrounding a plunger and a hollow clamping-frame, whereby the sheet will be gripped between the gripper and the hollow clamping-frame and be held taut and will be made to permanently conform to the shape of the face of the plunger, substantially as set forth.

In testimony whereof we have signed our names to this specification in the presence of two subscribing witnesses.

ALFRED C. HAFELY.
JENS REDLEFSEN.
CHARLES A. HAPPE.

Witnesses:
J. B. GUNN,
F. W. GREAVES.

(No Model.)

A. C. HAFELY, J. REDLEFSEN & C. A. HAPPE.

METHOD OF AND APPARATUS FOR VENEERING WITH CELLULOID COVERS AND CORNERS OF BOOKS, BOXES, &c.

No. 601,214. Patented Mar. 22, 1898.

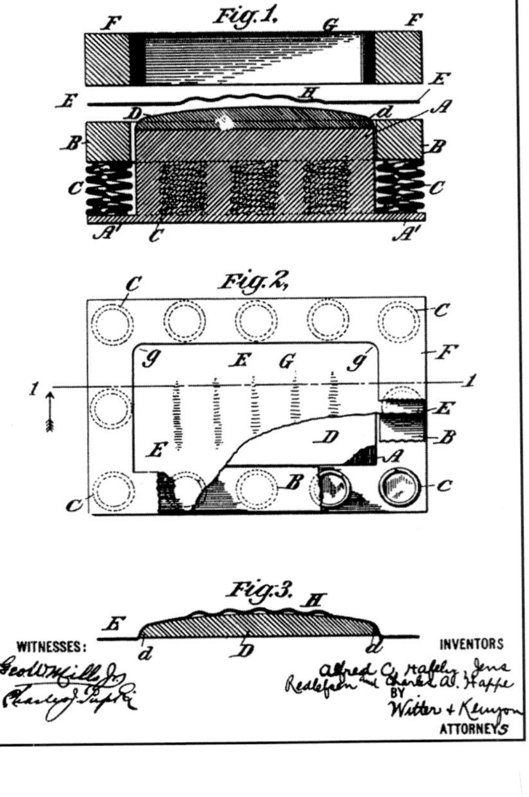
Fig. 1.
F
G
F
E
H
E
D
d
A
B
B
C
C
A'
C
A'
Fig. 2.
C
C
F
g
E
G
g
1
1
E
B
D
E
B
A
C
C
Fig. 3.
H
E
d
D
d
WITNESSES:
INVENTORS
BY
Witter + Kenyon
ATTORNEYS

Patents of miscellaneous items employing celluloid in their manufacture.

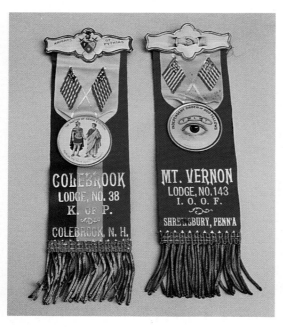

Reverse.

Left: Top part says Whitehead & Hoag Co., Newark, NJ. Right: Medallion says The Whitehead Hoag Co., Newark, NJ.

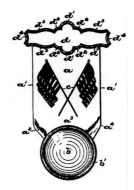

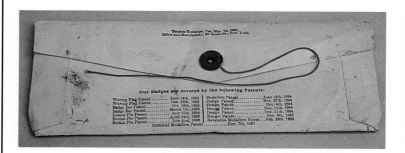

Envelope that badges came in.

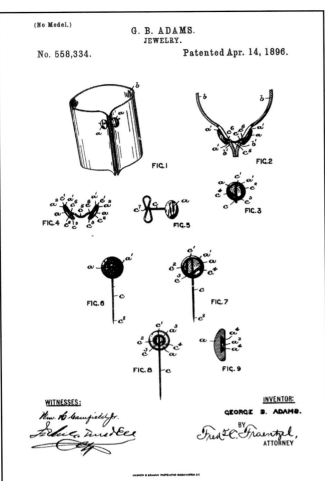

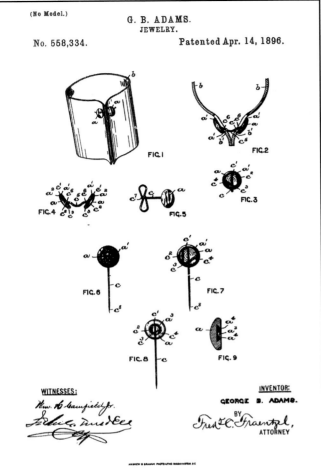

Stick pin.

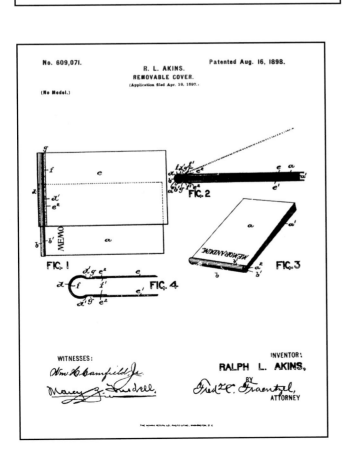

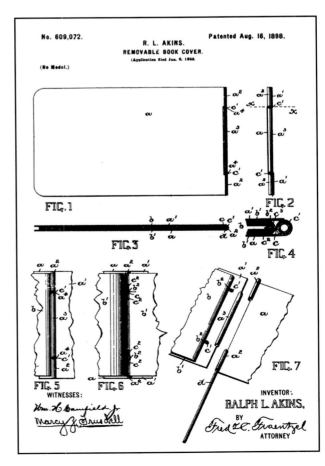

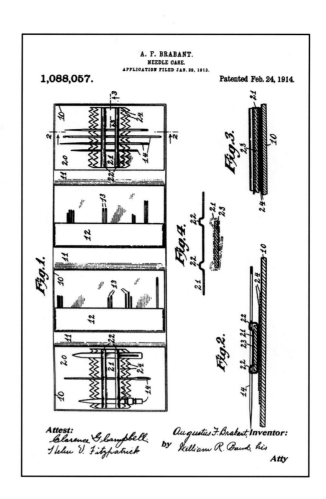

Celluloid-backed pocket mirrors were popular in the early 1900s and many can be found bearing advertisements. They can be found in round, oval, and rectangular shapes and can range in size from an inch and a half to as much as five inches wide. Many companies produced these wares in the United States. Whitehead and Hoag of Newark, New Jersey, is probably the most famous, but many were also manufactured by the Parisian Novelty Co. of Chicago and Bastian Brothers of Rochester, New York.

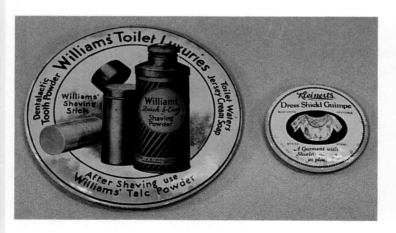

Advertising mirrors (mirror on reverse side), Left mirror 4½" wide. Right mirror 2" wide.

Novelty of Whitehead and Hoag Co. Celluloid piece is 2" in diameter.

It is not the intent of the authors to go into detail about every single patent for celluloid but rather to show the most important developments in its evolution.

Many wonderful books on plastics and celluloid have already been written and are listed in the bibliography. Serious researchers should refer to them for further information. The National Plastics Center and Museum, 210 Lancaster St., Rt. 117, P.O. Box 639, Leominster, Massachusetts, may also be contacted or visited for information.

Listed below are a number of known celluloid patents discovered by the authors.

Patent number	Inventor	Date	Invention
88,633	John W. Hyatt	4/6/1869	Improved molding composition to imitate ivory and other substances
91,341	John W. Hyatt and Isaiah Hyatt	6/15/1869	Improved method of making solid collodion
105,338	John W. Hyatt and Isaiah S. Hyatt	7/12/1870	Improvement in treating and molding pyroxyline
113,055	Isaiah Smith Hyatt John Wesley Hyatt Jesse A. Perkins	3/28/1871	Improvement in dental plates from pyroxyline
133,229	I. Smith Hyatt	11/19/1872	Improvement in processes and apparatus for manufacturing pyroxyline
152,232	John W. Hyatt	6/23/1874	Improvement in apparatus and processes for molding celluloids and the compounds of pyroxyline
156,352	I. Smith Hyatt John W. Hyatt	10/27/1874	Improvement in manufacturing solidified collodion
156,353	John W. Hyatt Isaiah S. Hyatt	10/27/1874	Improvement in the manufacture of celluloid
162,752	R. Finley Hunt	5/4/1875	Improvement in processes and apparatus for softening molding celluloid
202,441	John W. Hyatt	4/16/1878	Improvement in coating with celluloid
205,271	John W. Hyatt	6/25/1878	Manufacture of sheets of celluloid and other analogous plastic compositions
205,880	David Lockwood	7/9/1878	Improvement in strips for coating articles with celluloid and other plastic compositions
232,037	John W. Hyatt	9/7/1880	Manufacture of celluloid
233,851	Nathan Hart & Robert H. Bacon	11/2/1880	Decorating celluloid

Patent number	Inventor	Date	Invention
239,791	John W. Hyatt	4/5/1881	Process of and apparatus for molding celluloid, hard rubber, bonsilate, and analogous plastic materials
239,792	John W. Hyatt	4/5/1881	Applying designs to articles made of plastic material
239,794	John W. Hyatt	4/5/1881	Manufacture of a factitious material to imitate ivory
241,005	Nathan Hart & Robert A. Bacon	5/3/1881	Decorating celluloid
251,260	David Lockwood	12/20/1881	Manufacture of articles coated with celluloid, pyroxyline
270,538	Mortimer P. Bogart	1/9/1883	Combining celluloid with woven or knitted fabric
275,215	Isaiah S. Hyatt	4/3/1883	Process of manufacturing sheets of celluloid and other plastic material
278,321	Albert B. Diss	5/29/1883	Mold for forming articles of celluloid and other plastic materials
280,745	John W. Hyatt	7/3/1883	Press or mold for coating articles with celluloid
296,967	John W. Hyatt	4/15/1884	Art of manufacturing celluloid and other compounds of pyroxline
296,970	John W. Hyatt John H. Stevens William H. Wood	4/15/1884	Manufacture of celluloid and other compounds of pyroxyline
326,119	John W. Hyatt John Everding	9/15/1885	Process of making solid compounds from soluble nitrocellulose
383,272	Adolph Bensinger (Germany)	5/22/1888	Process of ornamenting celluloid surfaces
388,287	Emil Kipper	8/21/1888	Collar or cuff
392,794	Joseph R. France	11/13/1888	Process of manufacturing collars, cuffs
393,750	Joseph R. France	12/4/1888	Process of manufacturing collars, cuffs from pyroxyline compounds
393,751	Joseph R. France	12/4/1888	Manufacture of pyroxyline compounds
393,752	Joseph R. France	12/4/1888	Apparatus for the manufacture of celluloid and similar compounds

Patent number	Inventor	Date	Invention
393,753	Joseph R. France	12/4/1888	Process of manufacturing articles from compounds of pyroxyline
415,566	Frank Rowell	11/19/1889	Method of coating celluloid plates
421,367	William H. Wood George C. Gillmore	2/11/1890	Process of embossing sheets of celluloid
484,006	Alfred C. Hafely	10/11/1892	Method of making corners, covers, and like parts for books, boxes, and similar articles of celluloid or kindred material
484,527	B. S. Whitehead	10/18/1892	Badge
488,630	Alfred C. Hafely	12/27/1892	Method of making corners, covers, and like parts for books, boxes, and similar articles of celluloid or kindred material
493,003	B. S. Whitehead	3/7/1893	Badge
22,788 (design)	C. H. Fernald	9/19/1893	Celluloid sheet
505,462	Alfred C. Hafely Jens Redlefsen	9/26/1893	Manufacture of celluloid boxes
521,198	B. S. Whitehead	6/12/1894	Badge
23,817 (design)	B. S. Whitehead	11/27/1894	Badge
23,858 (design)	B. S. Whitehead	12/11/1894	Badge
23,859 (design)	B. S. Whitehead	12/11/1894	Badge
534,446	Horace E. Miller	2/19/1895	Machine for molding articles from plastic materials
535,039	B. S. Whitehead	3/5/1895	Badge
542,452	Charles H. Thurber Christian W. Schaefer	7/9/1895	Celluloid articles and process of manufacturing same
564,356	George B. Adams	7/21/1896	Badge pin or button
565,582	B. S. Whitehead	8/11/1896	Badge
570,442	G. B. Adams	11/3/1896	Key ring or the like
572,237	George B. Adams	12/1/1896	Stamp or coin case
580,102	G. B. Adams	4/6/1897	Scarf holder, garment supporter

Patent number	Inventor	Date	Invention
580,103	G. B. Adams	4/6/1897	Clamping or holding device
592,610	W. Hornick, Jr.	10/26/1897	Badge
595,853	A. J. Keil	12/21/1897	Badge
601,214	Alfred C. Hafely	3/22/1898	Method for apparatus for veneering with celluloid covers and corners of books, boxes
602,159	Edwin D. Harrison Charles H. Thurber	4/12/1898	Method of producing pyroxyline imitations of mosaic
605,185	Horace E. Miller	6/7/1898	Brush
607,104	B. S. Whitehead	12/12/1898	Device for displaying photographs, pictures
635,917	Charles F. Church	10/31/1899	Process of manufacturing articles covered with celluloid or like material
654,688	John Edward Thornton Charles Frederick Seymour Rathwell (England)	7/31/1900	Substitute for celluloid and process of manufacturing same
657,535	Carl Gustav Hageman Friedrich Otto Cornelius Zimmerman (Germany)	9/11/1900	Manufacture of celluloid
662,961	Ademor N. Petit	12/4/1900	Solvent material for treating surfaces of celluloid
667,600	George H. Stevens	2/3/1901	Molding celluloid
677,012	George Hillard Benjamin	6/25/1901	Art of manufacturing celluloid
699,516	Julius Hachenberg	5/6/1902	Manufacture of celluloid articles
803,952	George Edward Woodward	11/7/1905	Non-inflammable celluloid and process for the production thereof
831,488	Oskar Bruno Thieme (Germany)	9/18/1906	Method for producing celluloid like substances
857,387	Pascal Durando (France)	6/18/1907	Machine for manufacturing celluloid combs
893,634	Pascal Marino (England)	7/21/1908	Process for rendering celluloid uninnflammable and incombustible
894,108	Lucien Louis Bethisy (France)	7/21/1908	Manufacture of non-inflammable celluloid
962,877	Jonas W. Aylsworth	6/28/1910	Celluloid composition

Patent number	Inventor	Date	Invention
964,483	Thomas Bolas (England)	7/19/1910	Manufacture of celluloid or the like
1,153,596	Emile Bronnert (Germany)	7/14/1915	Non-inflammable celluloid-like mass and process of production thereof
1,164,821	William H. Kingston	12/21/1915	Manufacture of celluloid-covered articles
1,173,282	Robert D. Leary	2/29/1916	Celluloid receptacle
1,203,947	John N. Whitehouse	11/7/1917	Machine for making seamless celluloid articles
1,211,588	Edgar Josephson	1/9/1917	Process of treating celluloid
1,228,219	J. Komorous	5/29/1917	Structure comprising disk covered with flexible material (tape measure)
1,231,383	J. Komorous	6/26/1917	Powder receptacle
1,231,384	J. Komorous	6/26/1917	Powder receptacle
1,233,063	J. Komorous	7/10/1917	Container (tape measure)
1,237,352	Frederico Geo. Lundi & John McMillan (England)	8/21/1917	Impressing celluloid
1,244,676	Joseph Wilcox	10/30/1917	Method of making a celluloid article
1,257,541	Warren S. Sillcocks	2/26/1918	Composite celluloid sheet
1,310,071	William Gurry	7/15/1919	Machine for shaping and polishing articles of celluloid and the like
1,315,480	Henry Dreyfus (England)	9/9/1919	Manufacture of non-inflammable celluloid
1,320,767	J. Komorous	11/4/1919	Tape measure
1,322,631	Henry Segall	11/25/1919	Celluloid article of manufacture and method of producing the same
1,325,931	Henry Dreyfus (Switzerland)	12/23/1919	Manufacture of uninflammable celluloid
1,350,157	Frederick W. Horton	8/17/1920	Process for treating celluloid products

Artists, Decoration, and Techniques Featured on Celluloid Items

Many famous artists' works were displayed on the photo albums and boxes. *The Gleaners* was painted in 1857 by Jean Francois Millet. Millet had a deeply rooted respect for the rural laborers and he often painted gleaners, reapers, and woodcutters. Thousands of reproductions of this famous painting have been sold over the years and the celluloid items reflect what was popular at the time they were manufactured.

The Gleaners portrays three peasant women collecting the scanty remains of the harvest after it had been reaped. The gleaners are reduced to laboring over the slim pickings which have been left.

Millet (1814 – 1875) was a master painter. He was born in Normandy, France, and studied with several prominent artists. He retired to the countryside around Barbizon and devoted himself to the painting of peasant life upon which his fame is established.

The Gleaners is regarded as one of the masterpieces of the nineteenth century. The painting has a cool, golden light which gives dignity to the figures. It is a harsh social comment on the poor, peasant classes of the era.

This Gleaners autograph album was advertised in 1907 for $2.25 for a dozen, approximately $.19 each.

Millet painted *The Angelus* in 1859. In this oil painting two peasants are in the field giving thanks for their crops. In the Roman Catholic Church Angelus means prayer to the Virgin. *The Angelus* was one of Millet's favorite paintings. It appears to be a romantic veneration of peasant life and rural simplicity painted in soft colors. The dictionary describes Angelus as a prayer said at morning, noon, and evening in the Roman Catholic Church, a bell was rung to tell the time for this prayer. In *The Angelus*, Millet wanted to give an impression of the church bells ringing in the background. The two peasants, a man and a woman, hear the bells, they rise, stop work and, with eyes cast down, recite a prayer.

Thomas Gainsborough (1727 – 1788) was an English painter of portraits and landscapes. In the 1770s he painted many pictures of the rural poor. He was one of the most significant painters of his generation. In several old celluloid ads, Gainsborough "heads" are featured.

Other artists mentioned include Charles Dana Gibson and Howard Chandler Christy. Gibson immortalized the Gibson Girls who were inspired by the three famous Langhorn sisters, one of whom he married. The Gibson Girl fad, however, was pretty much over by 1908. Howard Christy (1873 – 1952) was an American painter and illustrator, best known for his creation of a feminine type, the Christy Girl.

Sir Edwin (Henry) Landseer (1802 – 1873) was one of the most highly respected and popular British painters of the nineteenth century. Animals remained the main subject of his art and he seemed to invest his animals with anthropomorphic qualities. A significant part of his output was deer and deer hunting. His painting *Monarch of the Glen*, circa 1851, was enormously popular and no doubt the box shown in the photo to the right is reminiscent of Landseer's work.

Maud Humphrey (1865 – 1940) was a painter and water-colorist specializing in portraits and child studies. She illustrated for *Harper's* and *Century* and other leading magazines. Maud was employed as a card designer and illustrator by Frederick A. Stokes Co. and Louis Prang & Co. until 1898 when she married Dr. Belmont Bogart. She was the mother of Humphrey Bogart. She collaborated with her sister, Mabel Humphrey on two miniature books published by Stokes Co.

Louis Prang (1824 – 1909) was born in Germany, came to New York City in 1850, and settled in Boston. He was self-taught and after a partnership with J. Mayer (1856 – 1860) opened his own lithographic firm in 1860 which became famous after the Civil War for its chromolithographic reproductions of famous paintings. He published popular drawing books and more than any other publisher of his time realized his great ambition of spreading art appreciation before the American public via the chromolithographs.

Frances I. Brundage was born in Newark, New Jersey, in 1854. She studied with her father, Rembrant Lockwood.

Photo album front cover has a chromolithograph signed Frances Brundage.

Paul De Longpre (1855 – 1911) was born in Lyons, France. He came to the United States in 1890. He was a self-taught artist, and at 12 years of age he was painting flowers on fans in Paris. At 21 his first oil painting was accepted at the Salon. In 1896 he gave his first exhibition in New York which consisted entirely of floral subjects. In 1899 he went to California and stayed until his death.

Alphonse Mucha was a famous poster artist. He was born in Prague in 1860. He studied in both Prague and Paris and often used Sarah Bernhardt as his model. He is known for his wonderful Art Nouveau style works. He came to live in the United States in the early 1900s.

Lillian Woolsey Hunter was a twentieth century painter and illustrator. She was a pupil of the H.B. Snell School in Cleveland and also the M. Walter School.

A number of the celluloid pieces have portraits of European nobility or famous women. Found are Queen Louise (1776 – 1810). Madame Juliette Recamier (1777 – 1849), and Anna Potocka (1776 – 1867).

Queen Louise had jet black hair, a whiteness of complexion, and was compared to a Greek statue. Napoleon felt she had a pretty face but little intelligence. Her people considered her a patriotic heroine. In 1793 at the age of 17 she captured the heart of Frederick William, heir to the throne of Prussia.

Madame Recamier was described by Napoleon as a brazen beauty and Anna Potocka was a Polish writer.

Many of the celluloid pieces have a so-called embossed design. Parts of the celluloid are raised up from the background. In 1890, William Wood and George Gillmore, assignors to the Celluloid Manufacturing Company in New York, New York, received patent #421,367 for the process of embossing sheets of celluloid.

The patent states "By means of our new method we are enabled with certainty and ease to emboss very thin sheets in either bold or delicate designs, and consequently produce the most beautiful and desirable patterns, applicable to panels, plaques, and other objects in great variety and at a low cost.

"The mold which we use consists of a die of metal and a force made of celluloid. To form this force, we simply mold in the die a sheet of seasoned celluloid sufficiently thick to correspond with the depth of the design, and to prevent the celluloid from flowing out of shape when heated we confine it in a metal ring or chase of a proper thickness. The force must be a perfect copy of the design, to effect which sometimes requires two or more moldings. By this means we not only obtain a force which is an exact counterpart of the die, but one which will flow under the heat and pressure used to emboss or mold the thin sheet of celluloid, and thereby force it into every part of the design."

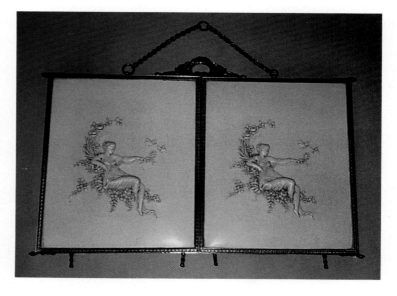

Hanging trifold mirror with white enamel type embossed design.

Josiah Wedgwood's popular Jasperware was in big demand during this time period and it is evident that some of the celluloid items were decorated in a similar fashion. The original ones featured cameos, portraits, raised figures, ornamental scrolls, and designs. This was done through the process of using liquid clay slip or sprigged-on-bas-relief. The celluloid pieces having this kind of decor are usually embossed to give this effect.

Celluloid Sets

Following is a list of possible contents found in sets (depending on the size of the set).

Smokers' set: pipe, cigar, and cigarette holders; match safe; and cigar cutter

Combination toilet and manicure cases: hand mirror, brush, comb, polisher, salve box, manicure scissors, cuticle knife, file, powder box, button hook, tweezers, nail brush, thimble, hatpin holder, jewel or button holder, perfume bottles

Jewel boxes/cases: some have compartments and jewel drawers with watch and ring holders, some have a tray, some a gilt lock and key

Shaving sets: some have a mirror in roof, bone handled and enameled bristle brushes, partition mug, some have a handled mirror, razor, comb, manicure scissors, razor holder, corn knife

Infants sets: comb, bone teething ring, soft bristle brush and metal powder box, infant's cup

Toilet case: brush, hand mirror, comb, some have mirror in roof

Work boxes/sewing boxes: some have mirror in roof, pincushion, thimble, scissors, threader, pick, some have jewelry drawer, some have hinged bar holders

Manicure set: polisher, salve box, file, button hook, tweezers, nail brush, cuticle knife, most utensils have bone handle fittings

Many of the different scenes and portraits found on the celluloid items are surrounded by floral designs. A few of the flowers that once adorned these items are apple blossoms, arbutus, dogwood, carnations, clematis, cherry blossoms, chrysanthemums, daisies, forget-me-nots, geraniums, iris, morning glories, pansies, poppies, primrose, sweet peas, tea roses, violets, water lilies, and wild roses.

Interior view of combination toilet and manicure case.

Interior view of shaving set.

Interior view of toilet case.

Interior view of collar & cuff box.

Interior view of jewel box/case.

Interior view of manicure case.

Inside of photo album.

Inside of autograph album — some have colored prints scattered throughout.

Interior linings have been described as:

Twilled mercerized lining
Moire puffed lining
Fine puffed satin lining
Mercerized puffed crepe lining
Puffed satin lining
Puffed twilled lining
Puffed watered lining

Puffed cloth lining
Puffed mercerized lining
Puffed mercerized twilled lining
Crepe lining
Cloth lining
Sateen lining
Colored mercerized lining

Exteriors have been described in the catalogs as:

Moire effect
Colored Oriental covering
Full celluloid
Leatherette bound
Plush bound
Mexican carved leather effect
Leather back
Imitation leather look
Woodgrain appearance
Double embossed celluloid
White enamel embossed design

Celluloid top over natural tinted pictures in gilt and floral frames
Gold scroll frame around medallion
Beaded gold metal frame around medallion
Embossed scroll and floral gilt frames
Etruscan gold corner ornaments
Embossed decorations
Spider web effect frames
Raised band edges under celluloid

Celluloid Jargon

Photo albums have different descriptions.

Regular upright type album.

CELLULOID LONGFELLOWS.
Nickel extension clasp, gold edge hinged leaves. Each in box.

F6076—7x16, asstd. red, blue and olive celluloid fronts with "Album" in gilt and colored bronze floral design, plush bound and back, nickel pinless clasp, gilt decorated tinted leaves with fly for 32 cabinets....Each, 72c

F6077—7¼x16, asstd. beautiful floral sprays, gilt and colored bronze embossed floral decorations, colored borders, silk plush bound, celluloid front and back, gilt pinless clasp, gilt floral decorated light gray leaves and fly for 48 cabinets......................Each, 98c

The longfellow.

HIGH GRADE STAND ALBUMS.
Domestic. Best sellers, heavily embossed gilt extension clasp, gold leaf edged leaves. Note number of leaves. Each in box.

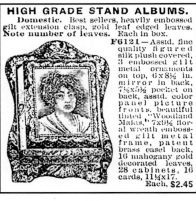

F6121—Asstd. fine quality figured silk plush covered, 3 embossed gilt metal ornaments on top, 6x8½ in. mirror in back, 7½x5½ pocket on back, asstd. color panel picture fronts, beautiful tinted "Woodland Maids," 7x9½ floral wreath embossed gilt metal frame, patent brass easel back, 16 mahogany gold decorated leaves, 28 cabinets, 16 cards, 11½x17. Each, $2.45

Stand album.

THE ORIGINAL "OX YOKE" EASEL ALBUMS.
Domestic—Guaranteed to be the best easel album made. Gold leaf edge hinged leaves, gilt extension clasps, newest designs, desirable colors, figured plush. All with 16 in. folding brass easels with hooks. Note number of leaves our books have. 1 in box.

F6115—Celluloid front over dainty natural color tinted fairy picture with embossed bands and silver ground decorated ends, 4 gilt embossed metal corners, asstd. colored figured plush backs, 16 mahogany gold decorated leaves, 52 cabinets, 5 carbonettes, 5 cards, 11½x9. Each, $1.35

Ox yoke easel album.

CELLULOID OBLONG PHOTO ALBUMS.
Extension pinless clasp, gold edge leaves. Each in box.

F6072—8¼x12, asstd. red, olive and blue fronts. "Album" embossed in gilt letters, gilt and colored bronze floral design, plush bound, gilt pinless clasp, gilt decorated tinted leaves with fly for 36 cabinets. Each, 75c

The oblong album.

Old catalog ads describe some of the box shapes. In an effort to have collectors refer to them by their original term the following pictures are shown:

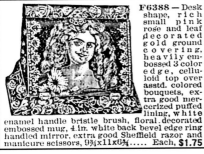

F6388 — Desk shape, rich small pink rose and leaf decorated gold ground covering, heavily embossed 3 color edge, celluloid top over asstd. colored bouquets, extra good mercerized puffed lining, white enamel handle bristle brush, floral decorated embossed mug, 4 in. white back bevel edge ring handled mirror, extra good Sheffield razor and manicure scissors, 9¾x11x6¾..... Each, $1.75

Desk shape.

F6579½ — "Good Luck" horseshoe shape, bevel plush covered extension base, pebbled ground, rich natural color floral decorated, tinted pictures under celluloid in gilt embossed frame, puffed mercerized lining, 4 pcs., polisher, salve box, file and nickel plated scissors, 6½x8¾x6½..... ....Set, 50c

Horseshoe (good luck) shape.

F6390 — Extraordinary $5.00 value. Swell sides, front and top, tinted wild rose sprays with foliage and buds, gold ground, asstd. landscape tops and fronts under celluloid, gilt frames, beveled extension base, extra quality puffed satin lining, cord trimmed, 4¼x7½ mirror in back, 6 pcs., bone handle bristle brush, partition china mug, gold edge and handle, floral decorated, 4 in. white back round beveled edge ring handle mirror, corn knife, white comb, warranted Sheffield razor, 9¾x20¾ x10¾................................ Each, $2.50

Swell sides.

F6430 — Acorn shape, full celluloid under new and artistic oriental effect bronze green and gold ground covering, cover with asstd. tinted flower girls in gold embossed frame, puffed satin lined, extra compartment for buttons, etc., 9x 10x12½. Each, $1.39

Acorn shape.

F6385 — Beveled extension base, asstd. large natural pink, red and tea roses, foliage background, dainty asstd. picture tops in rich colors under celluloid, 2 embossed gold bands, extra good mercerized lining, 5¾x7 mirror in top, enameled handle bristle brush, embossed scalloped edge, floral decorated china partition mug, 6½x10½x6¾.....Each, 95c

Beveled extension base.

F6568 — Heart shape, medallion picture and rose decorated top with gold scroll border under celluloid in beaded embossed gold frame, silk plush edges with 3 floral embossed gilt ornaments, rose wreath border around sides under celluloid with embossed edges, silk plush covered back, celluloid gold green and red trimmed bevel base, fine puffed satin lining, large painted gold trimmed decorated back hand mirror and brush, 2 salve boxes, polisher, comb, bone handle file, button hook, cuticle knife, nickeled scissors, 11¼x13x12. Each, $3.50

Heart shape.

Roll-top desk shape.

31

Care and Maintenance

The continual care and maintenance of the celluloid covered collectibles is a necessary and critical part of preventing future deterioration and preserving the value and beauty of these items. Think about the life of these collectibles, many are now 100+ years old. Some are still in perfect condition. Some are in various levels of deterioration. How did some items make it through 100 years in mint condition and some didn't? What actually started the deterioration of many pieces? A close examination shows indications that moisture was present at some point during the life of the item and we would speculate that moisture is the cause of most deterioration — moisture in the form of humidity. We generally think of moisture as liquid (water), however moisture in the form of humidity can have a very damaging effect on the celluloid covered items. The walls of the boxes are made of wood. The wood absorbs moisture thus causing expansion to the point of breaking the sealant along the edges and corners. Now the door is open for many types of deterioration. Additional moisture enters. The loosened area is snagged and torn, etc.

Some collectors offer different remedies and materials for the preservation of celluloid covered items and some of these are advisable, however, we offer the thought and suggestion that humidity might be our worst enemy. A reasonable climate controlled environment is probably the first step in the care of your celluloid covered collectibles. Storage in the hot dry attic or the damp basement is not the best place for these pieces.

Several collectors have recommended Armor All® for cleaning and protection of the finish. Armor All should not damage the celluloid but if applied too heavily there may be seepage through cracks or under loose edges resulting in damage to the pictures and prints. If Armor All is used, a very soft cloth slightly dampened with Armor All would be suggested. Never saturate the cloth to the point where liquid is being applied to the surface. A test spot should be tried first. The Armor All will leave a protective coating and return some of the original patina to the celluloid. Other collectors use Pledge® furniture polish and other mild non-abrasive polishes.

We again must ask the question, how did some of the celluloid covered items survive 100+ years and remain in perfect condition? We doubt if any chemicals were used during the lifetime of these items for the purpose of preservation. The condition is most likely due to the climatic environment in which it was stored. Some of the damage we find was the result of heat or sparks. The cigarette burn is one of the most common. One can only guess what caused some of the burn marks; sparks from a stove or fireplace, too much heat from heating stoves, carelessly placed matches and curling irons would probably be among the many reasons. Celluloid is flammable and will become very pliable when subjected to heat. Overheating will cause expansion and cracking. Again, this is an environmental problem. Hot lights, heating vents, stoves, TV sets, appliances can all be enemies of celluloid. It would not be wise to display your beautiful piece on top of the TV, for example.

Examples of pieces that are cracked and deteriorating. Try to avoid these types of items.

Some collectors suggest using cotton swabs dampened in detergent and water to clean around embossed areas. We offer this suggestion, however, caution against the use of moisture. The damage caused by moisture seeping through the slightest crack may not be realized immediately. Your beautiful piece may show deterioration years later and will never be connected to the attempt to clean the item.

Repair and Restoration

Antiques and collectibles begin losing value and desirability when altered, repaired, or reconstructed, however there may be cases when repair or restoration is advisable.

1. Resealing
2. Replacement of hardware

The celluloid covered boxes, albums, tri-fold mirrors, etc., of the Victorian era may occasionally require resealing especially along the edges of corners. When the celluloid cover begins to loosen or peel back along the edges it would be advisable to reseal these areas as opposed to leaving the edge loose and subject to further damage due to snagging or cracking. In most instances major damage to an item began when a small area became unsealed. The unsealed area received additional damage through improper handling, storage, or some other abuse until the once very minor and repairable area deteriorateded to a point of no hope, including missing and torn areas.

When resealing an area the utmost caution and care must be followed. Never be in a hurry.

Many glues will discolor the celluloid. Additional damage may occur when attempting to insert the glue under the celluloid. This is not an exact science. We can only offer suggestions and sympathy.

The unsealed area may require opening or raising the celluloid slightly, permitting the sealing agent to flow under and into the unsealed area. When attempting to lift the celluloid *never* use sharp metal instruments such as razor blades, pocket knives, or kitchen hardware. Always use wood, such as tooth picks and popsicle sticks, or plastic. The corner of an old credit card is an excellent tool for this operation. We have been more successful with a household grade clear contact cement Duro® by the Loctite Corporation. This cement will adhere to any surface and seems to be less likely to discolor the prints. The contact cement leaves a good seal along the edges. Any excess is easily wiped or pulled off with the fingers. Several collectors use the hot glue gun, clear household Goop®, and Duro® all purpose spray adhesive with varying degrees of success. Superglues and wood glues tend to discolor and do not adhere well. Always try a very small test area first. What works in one case may not work in another.

The replacement of the hardware (hinges, clasps, brackets, etc.) on the boxes and albums is a simple process. The difficult part is finding extra hardware which matches the piece being replaced. The only source of replacement parts is junk albums and boxes.

The hardware is attached with nails which can be pried and pulled out. The mounting flange of the hinge and clasp are very thin and will easily bend and tear so be gentle and take time to prevent damage. After removal, the hardware can be attached to another box or album by pressing the nails into place.

Reproductions

Although it is highly unlikely that boxes, photo albums, and tri-fold mirrors will be reproduced, it must be noted that the small pocket mirrors have been. At present they seem fairly easy to identify. They look newer in appearance but after a few years with some age on them they might get to be a bit of a problem.

Shown below are two legitimate vintage mirrors and a reproduction. The genuine mirrors are on the left and the right. Many patterns have been featured on the reproductions and collectors need to be alert. It has also been reported that some of the small tape measures have also been reproduced.

Celluloid Inventory Sheet

Collectors should always have a complete inventory of their celluloid collection, both photos and accompanying information. Since celluloid pieces vary from other collectibles, we have devised an inventory sheet that should allow you to note all significant information.

Photocopy* this sheet and insert copies in a three-ring binder. Your current collection can be kept in the front part and items that have been sold in the back. Whenever items match pieces shown in *Celluloid Collectibles of the Victorian Era*, be sure to make a notation. Reappraise your items every few years and update these prices on your inventory sheet.

*Permission is given by the authors to photocopy the inventory sheet for the PERSONAL use of collectors only.

CELLULOID INVENTORY SHEET

PLACE PHOTO HERE

Item(s)_____

Date Acquired_____

Purchased From_____

Price Paid $_____

Description (height, width, diameter, etc.)

_____

_____

_____

Celluloid Treasures of the Victorian Era
Reference #:

If exact item, plate #_____

If not exactly as shown:

Similar shape, plate #_____

Similar pattern or design, plate #_____

Additional Information _____

_____

Condition _____

_____

Other:

Current appraisals:

Date _____ Value $ _____

Date _____ Value $ _____

Date _____ Value $ _____

Date _____ Value $ _____

Date Sold _____

Selling Price _____

Sold To _____

Old Ads

Butler Bros. & Sears catalogs 1900 – 1909.

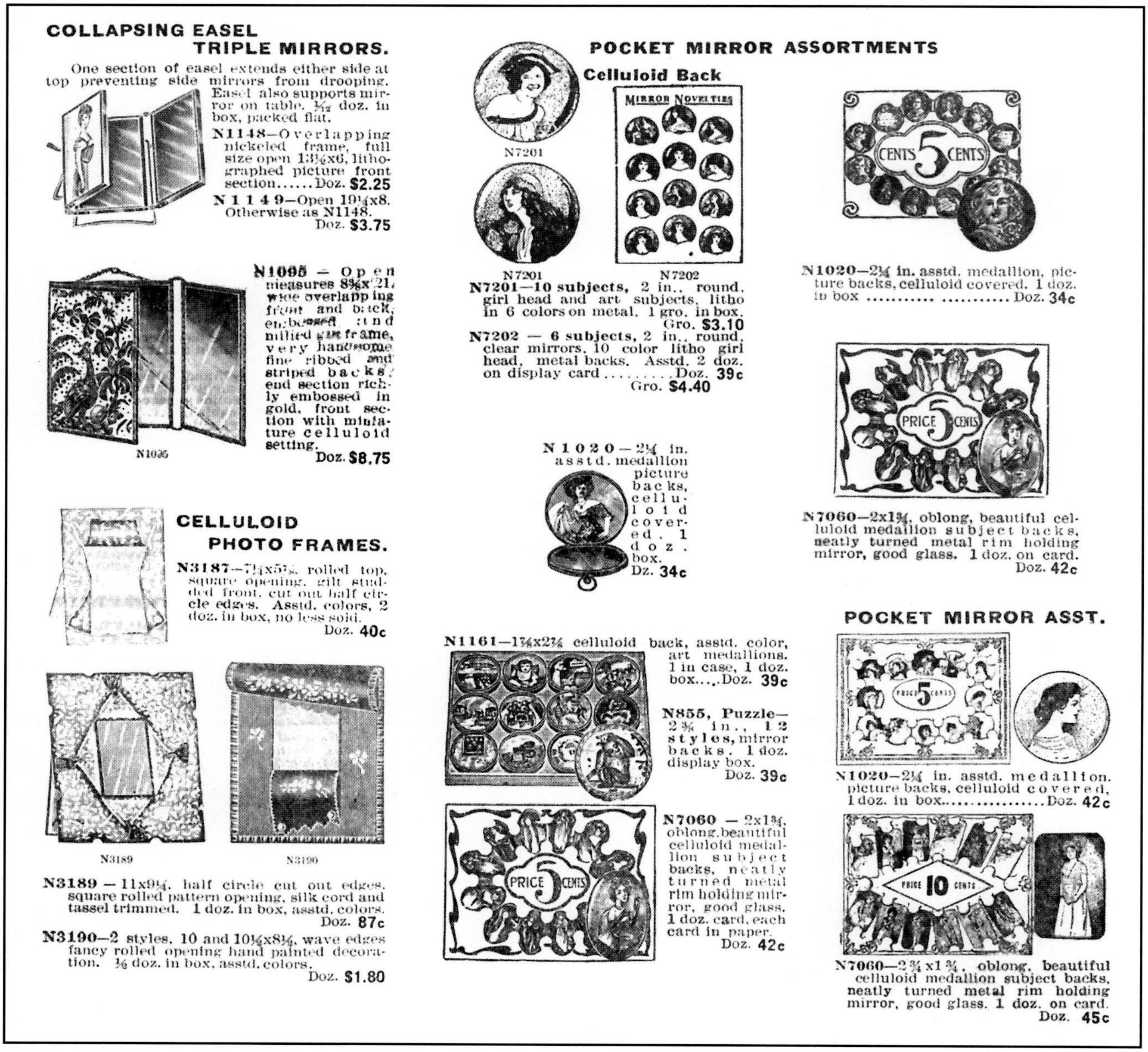

COLLAPSING EASEL TRIPLE MIRRORS.

One section of easel extends either side at top preventing side mirrors from drooping. Easel also supports mirror on table. 1/12 doz. in box, packed flat.

N1148—Overlapping nickeled frame, full size open 13⅛x6, lithographed picture front section......Doz. **$2.25**

N1149—Open 19¼x8. Otherwise as N1148. Doz. **$3.75**

N1095

N1095 — Open measures 8⅜x21, wide overlapping front and back, embossed and milled gilt frame, very handsome fine ribbed and striped backs; end section richly embossed in gold, front section with miniature celluloid setting. Doz. **$8.75**

CELLULOID PHOTO FRAMES.

N3187—7¼x5⅞, rolled top, square opening, gilt studded front, cut out half circle edges. Asstd. colors, 2 doz. in box, no less sold. Doz. **40c**

N3189 N3190

N3189 — 11x9¼, half circle cut out edges, square rolled pattern opening, silk cord and tassel trimmed. 1 doz. in box, asstd. colors. Doz. **87c**

N3190—2 styles, 10 and 10⅛x8¼, wave edges fancy rolled opening hand painted decoration. ⅙ doz. in box, asstd. colors. Doz. **$1.80**

POCKET MIRROR ASSORTMENTS

Celluloid Back

N7201 N7201 N7202

N7201—10 subjects, 2 in., round, girl head and art subjects, litho in 6 colors on metal. 1 gro. in box. Gro. **$3.10**

N7202 — 6 subjects, 2 in., round, clear mirrors, 10 color litho girl head, metal backs. Asstd. 2 doz. on display card.........Doz. **39c** Gro. **$4.40**

N1020—2¼ in. asstd. medallion, picture backs, celluloid covered. 1 doz. in box ....Doz. **34c**

N1020—2¼ in. asstd. medallion picture backs, celluloid covered. 1 doz. box. Dz. **34c**

N7060—2x1¾, oblong, beautiful celluloid medallion subject backs, neatly turned metal rim holding mirror, good glass. 1 doz. on card. Doz. **42c**

N1161—1⅞x2⅞ celluloid back, asstd. color, art medallions. 1 in case, 1 doz. box....Doz. **39c**

N855, Puzzle—2¾ in., 12 styles, mirror backs. 1 doz. display box. Doz. **39c**

N7060 — 2x1¾, oblong, beautiful celluloid medallion subject backs, neatly turned metal rim holding mirror, good glass. 1 doz. card, each card in paper. Doz. **42c**

POCKET MIRROR ASST.

N1020—2¼ in. asstd. medallion. picture backs, celluloid covered, 1 doz. in box..................Doz. **42c**

N7060—2¾x1¾, oblong, beautiful celluloid medallion subject backs, neatly turned metal rim holding mirror, good glass. 1 doz. on card. Doz. **45c**

DOMESTIC STAND ALBUMS.

The best selling numbers from the leading manufacturers of high grade albums. All with heavy embossed extension gilt clasps, gold leaf edged leaves. 1 in box.

F6121—Fine asstd. figured silk plush covered, 3 large embossed gilt metal ornaments on top, 6¾x8¾ mirror in back, 7½x5 pocket on back, asstd. colored medallion picture fronts under celluloid in embossed gilt frame, 16 mahogany gold decorated leaves, 24 cabinets, 4 carbonettes, 16 cards, 11¼x17. Each, **$2.38**

MUSICAL ALBUMS.

Gilt pinless extension clasps, gilt edged, gilt decorated beveled leaves and fly. Each plays two airs, wound by attached keys.

F6093

F6094

F6093—9x11, asstd. 3 shades, 2 color fronts, celluloid, embossed "Album," scroll in gilt and color, plush bound, metal corners and feet, steel gray leaves for 22 carbonettes, 8 cards.......................... Each, **$1.75**

F6094—Floral picture, gilt and colored frame, shaded border and base, gilt corners and clasp. 14 gilt decorated tinted leaves and fly for 29 cabinets................Each, **$2.25**

F6095 — 10x12½, green tinted front with landscape and village, embossed gilt and hand painted enamel floral frame, plush bound, celluloid base, gilt corners and feet, 14 mahogany double leaves for 51 cabinets, 12 cards. Each, **$3.00**

F6095

F6094—9¼x11, asstd. beautiful floral pictures, gilt and colored bronze embossed floral and scroll frame, colored border, under celluloid, silk plush bound and base with embossed metal corners and feet, heavy embossed gilt pinless clasp, 14 gilt scroll decorated tinted leaves and fly for 29 cabinets. Each, **$2.25**

F6095 — 10x12½, green tinted front with landscape and village, embossed gilt and hand painted enamel floral frame, heavy gilt embossed pinless clasp, plush bound, celluloid base, gilt corners and feet, 14 mahogany double leaves for 51 cabinets, 12 cards........................Each, **$3.00**

ALBUMS.

Musical—9 x 11, 2 colors, celluloid landscapes, embossed floral sprays in gold and colors, plush bound, metal corners, tinted leaves for 22 cabinets, 8 cards. Plays 2 airs, attached key, gilt pinless extension clasps, lacquered gilt edges, leaves and fly.
J734—1 in box. Each, **$2.35**

MUSICAL ALBUMS.

Gilt pinless extension clasps, gilt edged, gilt decorated beveled leaves and fly. Each plays two airs, wound by attached keys. Each in box.

F6094

CELLULOID LONGFELLOWS.

Nickel extension clasp, gold edge hinged leaves. Each in box.

F6076

F6077

F6076—7x16, asstd. red, blue and olive celluloid fronts with "Album" in gilt and colored bronze floral design, plush bound and back, nickel pinless clasp, gilt decorated tinted leaves with fly for 32 cabinets....Each, **72c**

F6077—7½x16, asstd. beautiful floral sprays, gilt and colored bronze embossed floral decorations, colored borders, silk plush bound, celluloid front and back, gilt pinless clasp, gilt floral decorated light gray leaves and fly for 48 cabinets.......................Each, **98c**

CELLULOID LONGFELLOWS.

EExtension clasp, gilt edge hinged leaves. 1 in box.

F6076

F6077

F6076—7x16, asstd. red, blue and olive fronts with "Album" in gilt and colored bronze floral design, plush bound and back, nickel pinless clasp, gilt decorated tinted leaves with fly for 32 cabinets....Each, **72c**

F6078

F6077—7x16, asstd. beautiful floral sprays, gilt and colored bronze embossed tinted borders, plush bound, celluloid back, gilt pinless clasp, gilt decorated gray leaves with fly for 48 cabinets. Each, **98c**

F6078—7x16, asstd. pictures, "Colonial Dames" gilt and colored bronze floral designs, mottled celluloid border, celluloid back, gilt pinless clasp, gilt decorated gray bevel leaves with fly for 48 leaves.....Each, **$1.30**

TRIPLICATE TOILET AND SHAVING MIRRORS.

Compare sizes very carefully when noting prices. 1/12 doz. in box, with chain hanger.

N1143—3 hinged metal frame mirrors, turned edges, asstd. enameled colors, colored picture backs, each 3x4, full size open 4x10⅝. 1 doz. in carton. Doz. **87c**

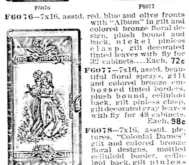

TOILET MIRROR OFFFRING.

A leader if you wish, a profit maker if you prefer.

N1144—3 part nickeled metal frame mirrors, 4⅛x6, full size open 6 x 13½, lithographed picture backs. ½ doz. in carton. Per dozen. **$1.90**

N1145—Open measures 19x8 in., otherwise as N1144. ¼ doz. in pkg. ....Doz. **$3.60**

N1146—Open measures 22¼x9, otherwise as N1144.........................Doz. **$5.25**

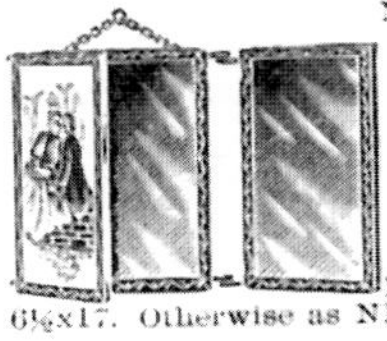

N1093—3 part hinged mirror, gilt, wide overlapping frame, embossed and milled design, excellent glass, full size open 5⅝x13½, leatheriod and lithographed picture backs. Doz. **$3.60**

N1094—Full size, open 6⅛x17. Otherwise as N1093........Doz. **$5.75**

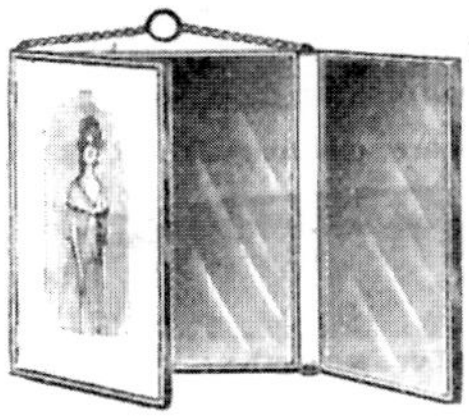

N1123—3 part nickeled overlapping metal frame, 8x10, full size open 10x24, excellent clear glass, lithographed female figures, floral and picture decorated backs. Doz. **$5.75**

N1095—Open measures 8¾x21, wide overlapping front and back, embossed and milled gilt frame, very handsome fine ribbed and striped backs, end section richly embossed in gold, front section with miniature celluloid setting. Doz. **$8.75**

N1096—With beveled heavy glass, size open 8¾x21, variety of backs in leather and other effects, end sections elaborately gilt embossed, one of which is set with celluloid miniature....Each, **$1.45**

IMPERIAL CELLULOID PHOTO ALBUMS—Quarto.

Extension clasp, gilt edge hinged leaves. 1 in box.

F6067

F6068

F6067—9½x12, asstd. landscapes in gilt and colored bronze and spider web effect frame, colored back, plush bound and corners, green tinted double leaves with fly for 40 cabinets........ ....Each, **73c**

F6068—9x14, large colored medallion picture, gilt embossed frame on asstd. shaded ground, plush bound and corners, nickel pinless clasp, tinted double leaves for 48 cabinets. Each, **85c**

F6063

F6064

F6063—8½x10½, celluloid front and back cover, asstd. floral sprays, landscapes in embossed frame of gilt and colored bronze, gilt pinless clasp, 16 gilt decorated gray leaves with fly for 28 carbonettes and 16 cards.............................Each, **98c**

F6064—8½x10½, asstd. beautiful pictures in artistic frame, rose decoration on gilt ground under celluloid cover, plush bound and padded back, gilt pinless clasp, 16 gilt decorated bevel tinted leaves with fly, 28 cabinets and 16 cards....Each, **$1.20**

F6065

F6065— 8½x10½, chrysanthemum floral design in asstd. colors on imit. back ground under celluloid front and back, medallion pictures in white enamel embossed frame, gilt pinless clasp, 16 gilt decorated bevel leaves with fly, 28 cabinets and 16 cards.. .Each, **$1.30**

THE ORIGINAL "OX YOKE" EASEL ALBUMS.

Domestic—Guaranteed to be the best easel album made. Gold leaf edge hinged leaves, gilt extension clasps, newest designs, desirable colors, figured plush. All with 16 in. folding brass easels with hooks. **Note number of leaves our books have.** Each in box.

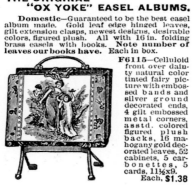

F6115—Celluloid front over dainty natural color tinted fairy picture with embossed bands and silver ground decorated ends, 4 gilt embossed metal corners, asstd. colored figured plush backs, 16 mahogany gold decorated leaves, 52 cabinets, 5 carbonettes, 5 cards, 11½x9. Each, **$1.38**

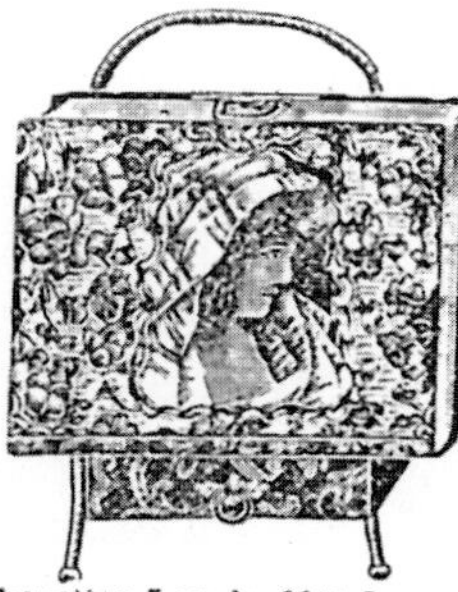

F6118—Asstd. color shaded figured plush back, celluloid front over dainty color asstd. pictures in embossed gold frame, clouded ground and natural color violet and leaf gold trim clouded ground border, 4 gilt metal corners, plush front drawer 6¼x7½ with metal pull, 16 mahogany gold decorated leaves, 52 cabinets, 5 carbonettes, 5 cards, 11½x9...........Each, **$1.85**

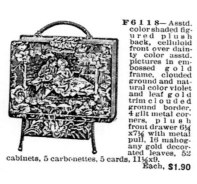

F6118—Asstd. color shaded figured plush back, celluloid front over dainty color asstd. pictures in embossed gold frame, clouded ground and natural color violet and leaf gold trim clouded ground border, 4 gilt metal corners, plush front drawer 6¼x7½ with metal pull, 16 mahogany gold decorated leaves, 52 cabinets, 5 carbonettes, 5 cards, 11½x9. Each, **$1.90**

BRASS OX YOKE EASEL ALBUMS.

Fine quality lacquered gold leaf edge, section hinged leaves, gilt clasp, attractive colors, plush and celluloid combination fronts, 15 in. folding brass easel. 1 in box.

J739—10¾x16½, figured silk plush, 3 embossed gilt ornaments, when open discloses 6½x8½ mirror back, 8x10½ tinted colonial picture panel front, brass handle, 10 gold edged floral decorated leaves, embossed gilt extension clasp. Holds 16 cabinets. 16 card photos..Each, **$1.85**

BRASS "OX YOKE" EASEL ALBUM.

Domestic—Guaranteed to be the best easel album made. Gold leaf edge hinged leaves, gilt extension clasp, newest designs, desirable colors, figured plush. All with 15 in. folding brass easels with hooks. **Note number of leaves our books have.**

3F6115—Celluloid front over dainty natural colored asstd. fairy pictures, embossed bands and frames, asstd. rich floral decorated backgrounds, 4 gilt embossed metal corners, asstd. color figured plush backs, 16 mahogany gilt decorated leaves, 52 cabinets, 5 carbonettes, 5 cards, 9x11½. 1 in box. Each, **$1.38**

CELLULOID OBLONG PHOTO.

Extension pinless clasp, gilt edge hinged leaves. 1 in box.

F6072—8½x12, asstd. red, olive and blue fronts, "Album" embossed in gilt letters, gilt and colored bronze floral design, plush bound, gilt pinless clasp, gilt decorated tinted leaves with fly for 36 cabinets ....Each, **75c**

F6073—8½x12, 2 designs, colored medallion pictures in gilt and floral frames, red, olive and blue border and celluloid back, plush bound, gilt pinless clasp, gilt decorated gray leaves with fly for 48 cabinets.... ....Each, **92c**

CELLULOID OBLONG PHOTO ALBUMS.

Extension pinless clasp, gold edge leaves. Each in box.

F6072—8½x12. asstd. red, olive and blue fronts. "Album" embossed in gilt letters, gilt and colored bronze floral design, plush bound, gilt pinless clasp, gilt decorated tinted leaves with fly for 36 cabinets. Each, 7[illegible]

HIGH GRADE STAND ALBUMS.

Domestic. Best sellers, heavily embossed gilt extension clasp, gold leaf edged leaves. **Note number of leaves.** Each in box.

F6121—Asstd. fine quality figured silk plush covered, 3 embossed gilt metal ornaments on top, 6x8½ in. mirror in back, 7½x5½ pocket on back, asstd. color panel picture fronts, beautiful tinted "Woodland Maids," 7x9½ floral wreath embossed gilt metal frame, patent brass easel back, 16 mahogany gold decorated leaves, 28 cabinets, 16 cards, 11½x17. Each, **$2.45**

A TOP NOTCHER.

Looks worth double this price.

F6125—Asstd. superior quality figured silk plush padded front, asstd. dainty medallion heads under celluloid in large oval embossed gilt metal frame, 4 metal corners, fancy metal scroll top and frame with landscape medallion under celluloid, 6x8 mirror in back, 7½x5½ pocket on back, patent brass easel, 18 mahogany gold trimmed leaves, 56 cabinets, 4 carbonettes, 12 cards, 12x17. Each, **$2.90**

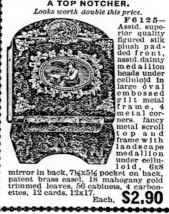

NOVELTY SILK AND SATIN BOXES WITH CELLULOID TOPS.

A dainty attractive line to sell at popular prices. This season's values better than ever. Each has silk or satin ribbon bow tyings and hand painted natural color floral decorated celluloid tops. All packed 1 in box, except F6250.

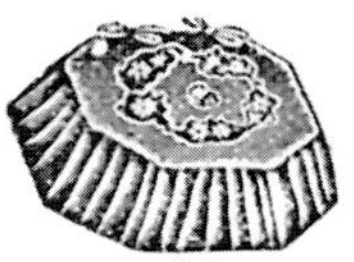

F6250

F6251

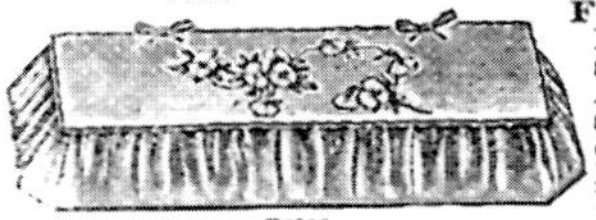

F6252

F6250—Puffed silk sides. Asstd. square, oblong, heart and hexagon, good size. 6 in box, asstd.................Each, **18c**

F6251 — Handkerchief or utility. 6½x6½, full puffed sides, crimped gilt edge tops. Each, **18c**

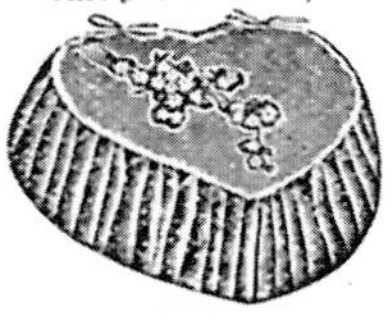

F6253

F6252 — Glove or necktie, 11½x5, matches F6251. Each, **18c**

F6253—Jewel, handkerchief or utility, heart shape, 7½x7¼, puffed silk sides, crimped gilt edge top...Each, **36c**

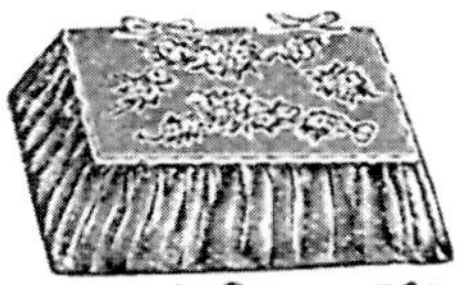

F6254—Handkerchief or utility, 8x7, puffed mercerized silk sides, puffed lining, crimped gilt edge top. Each, **36c**

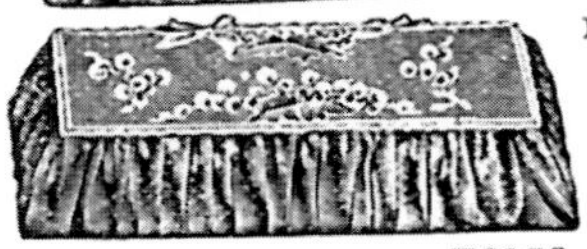

F6255—Glove or necktie, 11½x5½, matches F6254. Each, **36c**

F6256—Exceptional dollar value. Handkerchief, jewel or utility, 8x8, satin puffed sides, satin lining, large double satin bow tyings, crimped gilt edge, satin finish celluloid top..Each, **★39**

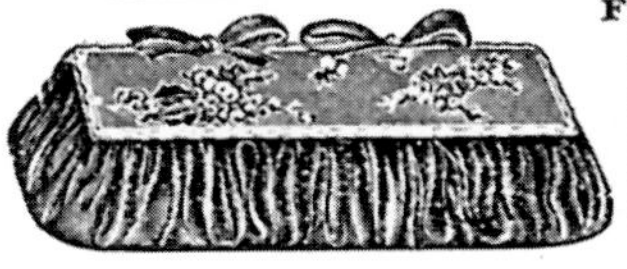

F6257—Glove, necktie or ribbon, 12x6, matches F6256. Each, **52c**

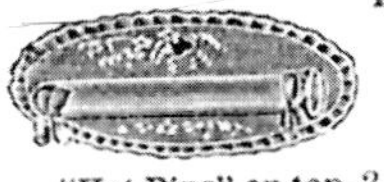

F6228, Hat Pin Holder—Moire wreath embossed ground, satin finish and asstd. colored crimped gold edge celluloid hand painted floral front, lettered "Hat Pins" on top. 2 silk ribbon bows with hanger, blown glass receptacle. 7¾x4¼. 1/12 doz. in box...... ....Doz. **$1.75**

F6229, Jewel, Hdkf. or Work Box—Full celluloid asstd. pink, blue and red corrugated sides, embossed and fluted top with ribbon bow hinges, hand painted floral decorated cover with "Jewels" etc., 3 metal brass feet, puffed embossed lining, 7¾x7¼. 1 in box..Each, **36c**

F6230, Novelty Jewel or Button Holder—Full celluloid asstd. pink, blue and transparent red, satin finish, fluted gold edge, turned corners, high art tinted picture in center, 2 compartments, one covered ribbon bow hinged, neat hand painted floral decorated, 11x6. 1 in box........ ....Each, **37c**

CELLULOID POST CARD CASES.

Bound to be big sellers. All with gilt metal clasps and hinges and puffed mercerized lining in top. Sizes given are with cases open. Each in box.

F6499

F6500

F6499—Richly tinted water lily and leaf decoration on water shaded blue ground, asstd. picture tops, extension base and top, neatly lined, ribbon lift. 4¾x6½x8........Each, **16c**

F6500—Natural color floral decorated bronze-green ground, embossed edge, puffed mercerized lined lid, celluloid top over tinted landscape scenes in embossed frames, 4¾x7¼x8¼...... ....Each, **31c**

F6501 — Artistically shaded iris & foliage decorated clouded gold ground, embossed edge, celluloid top over asstd. "Sunbonnet Series" pictures, mercerized puffed lined lid, 2 compartments with ribbon lifts, 8½x7¾x8¼..............................Each, **65c**

A HANDSOME CASE.

Mighty profitable for the merchant, too.

F6503 — Natural color small pink roses with foliage gold & bronze green covering, embossed edge, full celluloid top, asstd. colored postal scenes, "Post Cards" in gilt embossed frame, puff mercerized lined top, 4 compartments, 12½x9½x10¼. Each, **$1.00**

F6506—Cabinet, embossed edge celluloid top and cover over asstd. colored pictures on top and front, embossed bronze green frame, beveled extension base, beautiful red poppy decoration on gold ground, puffed mercerized lined lid, 2 compartments, 8¾x5x8½........ ....:.Each, **75c**

F6506—Cabinet, neat asstd. colored gold trimmed floral decorated light blue back, ground covering, beveled extension base, gold decorated floral embossed edge, celluloid front and top with asstd. colored pictures in embossed gold frame and colored post cards in front. 2 compartments. 9x7x7½ .....Each. **75c**

CELLULOID PHOTO CASES.

Growing more popular each year. All with gilt clasps except F6485. Sizes given are with cases open. Each in box, unless specified.

F6485

F6486

F6485—Asst. colored morning glory and leaf decorated coloring, lid with medallion pictures in embossed frame, "Photo" embossed on top, neatly lined, 5¼ x 7¼ x 8¾. 3 in box, asstd...........................Each, **17c**

F6486—Natural color delicate arbutus floral and leaf decorated clouded blue moire ground covering, asstd. tinted pictures in red enameled and gold embossed frame, ribbon scroll top, puffed mercerized satin lining, ribbon lift, 5½x9x10.............Each, **33c**

F6486

F6486—Rich large pink yellow and white rose and leaf decorated covering, medallion picture in embossed frame on top, neatly lined ribbon lift, 5⅜ x 8¾ x 9¾. Each, **33c**

F 6491 --Bronze green and gold ground asstd. colored floral decorated covering, cured edge base, embossed edge celluloid top with figured plush ends, asstd. medallion pictures in gold embossed frame, puffed satin lining, ribbon lift, diamond embossed gilt frame mirror in roof, 10½x9¾x9¾. Each, **$1.25**

F6489 — Rich pink, white and yellow rose and leaf decorated watered effect bronze green and gold ground covering, embossed edge celluloid top with high art asstd. tinnted figures in gold embossed frames, puffed satin lining, ribbon lift, 8½ x 8½ x 8¾ ....Each, **79c**

F6490 —Rich maroon gold figured ground natural colored floral decorated covering, bevel edge base, celluloid top and front, asstd. medallion pictures in fancy embossed gold frame, fine puffed satin lining, ribbon lift, 9½x8¾x9¾ Each, **95c**

F6488 — Dainty small pink rose and leaf decorated bronze green and gold ground covering, curved edge base, celluloid embossed edge top over asstd. colored medallion pictures, puffed mercerized lining, ribbon lift, diamond mirror in roof, 8⅛x7¾x3¾....................Each, **72c**

F6496—Shaded white pink and yellow rose and leaf on dark ground covering, gold embossed edge celluloid front and top over asstd. natural tinted pictures, puffed watered effect lining, 10⅜x4½x8½.........Each, $1.20

CELLULOID CABINET PHOTO HOLDERS.

Each with bevel extension base, fancy embossed gilt clasp and hinges. 1 in box.

F6495—Beautiful natural color floral decorated dark blue ground, gold embossed edge, celluloid top and front over asstd. tinted pictures, fine quality mercerized puffed lining, 6¾x8¼x4½........Each, 73c

F6496—Exquisite arum lilies with leaves and buds on dark ground covering, embossed gold & bronze-green edged celluloid top and front overlaid-ty tinted pictures and large bouquets flowers, puffed mercerized lining, 10⅜x8½x4½..................Each, $1.10

IMPERIAL CELLULOID PHOTO ALBUMS.

Extension clasp, gold edge hinged leaves. Each in box.

F6067

F6067—9⅛x11¾, asstd. shaded fronts and backs, landscapes in gilt embossed frame with scroll and floral gilt and colored bronze decorations, asstd. plush bound and corners, tinted floral gilt decorated leaves, double open: ...r 40 cabinets..Each, 73c

F6062

F6062— 8½x10½, mottled and shaded celluloid cover, "Album" and floral design in gilt and colored bronze, figured plush back, gilt pinless clasp, 16 gilt decorated tinted leaves with fly for 28 carbonettes and 16 cards......Each, 82c

F6061

F6061—2 designs, 8½x10½, asstd. floral and landscape scenes in gilt and colored bronze embossed floral frames, plush bound celluloid front and colored backs, gilt pinless clasp, 14 gilt floral decorated light green leaves and fly for 24 carbonettes and 16 cards. Each, 78c

F6063—8½x10½, asstd. floral and landscape scenes, gilt and colored bronze corners, plush bound, celluloid front and back, fancy gilt clasp, 16 scroll and floral gilt decorated tinted leaves and fly for 28 carbonettes and 16 cards. Each, $1.00

F6064

F6064—8½x10½, medallion Asti heads in artistic floral and scroll embossed gilt frame on gilt ground, natural carnation background under celluloid, figured plush bound and back, gilt pinless clasp, 16 gold decorated tinted leaves for 28 cabinets and 16 cards....Each, $1.20

F6052

F6052—7x8¼, 4 styles, shaded fronts, colored chromo picture in embossed gilt frame, gilt and colored bronze floral spray embossing, 2 with "Album" in gilt and colored floral spray design, pinless clasp, 10 tinted leaves and fly for 18 cabinets and 4 cards. 4 in pkg............Each, 30c

F6053

F6054

F6053—4 styles, 7x8⅝, asstd. solid and shaded tints, 2 with "Album" in gilt, embossed floral and gilt decorations; 2 with landscape scenes, floral decorated, plush bound and corners, nickel clasp, 10 tinted leaves with fly for 16 cabinets, 8 cards. 4 in pkg., asstd. Each, 33c

F6054—2 styles, 7¾x10, asstd. shaded fronts and solid backs, embossed gilt and colored bronze floral design, "Album" and medallion picture with floral bands, 9 steel gray leaves with fly for 16 carbonettes and 4 cards. 2 in pkg........Each, 38c

F6053

F6053—4 styles, 7x8⅝, asstd. solid and shaded tints, 2 with floral and landscape scenes, 2 with "Album" in gilt, embossed gilt and colored bronze floral decorations, celluloid front and back, plush bound and corners, 10 asstd. decorated tinted leaves with fly for 16 cabinets and 8 cards...............Each, 33c

F6054

F6055

F6054—8x10, 2 styles, asstd. shaded fronts, solid backs, embossed gilt "Album" with colored bronze floral designs, asstd. medallion pictures in gilt frames, plush bound and corners, 9 gold floral decorated steel gray leaves with fly for 16 cabinets and 4 cards. 2 in pkg............................Each, 38c

F6055—7¾x10, asstd. shaded fronts, colored medallion pictures, 2 styles in gilt embossed floral and scroll frame, plush bound and corners, nickel extension clasp, 12 tinted decorated leaves with fly for 20 cabinets and 16 cards. 2 in pkg. Each, 50c

F6087

F6087—Figured silk plush, asstd. colors, full size 4 etruscan gold corner ornaments, colored picture under celluloid, gilt pinless clasp, 16 gilt decorated tinted leaves and fly for 16 carbonettes, 12 cabinets and 16 cards. Each, $1.25

F6087

F6087—Figured silk plush, asstd. colors, full size 4 etruscan gold corner ornaments, colored picture under celluloid, gilt pinless clasp, 16 gilt decorated tinted leaves and fly for 16 carbonettes, 12 cabinets and 16 cards. Each, $1.25

F6057

F6057—3 style children pictures, gilt embossed frame, tinted front and back, 8½x10¾, plush bound and corners, nickel pinless clasp, 14 gilt decorated gray leaves with fly for 24 carbonettes and 16 cards.......Each, 62c

F6058

F6060

F6058—"Cowboy" girl picture, 2 designs, gilt and colored bronze floral embossed shaded front, plush bound and corners, pinless clasp, 16 gilt decorated leaves with fly for 28 carbonettes and 16 cards . ....Each, 67c

F6060—Shaded light green fronts, 8½x10¾, embossed "Album", gilt and colored floral design, silk plush bound and corners, tinted celluloid back, gilt pinless clasp, 16 gilt decorated gray leaves and fly for 28 carbonettes and 16 cards......Each, 75c

COMBINATION CELLULOID TOILET & MANICURE CASES.

All with hinged covers, gilt clasps, fittings on spring holders; fancy embossed back brush and mirror. Brush genuine bristle. Sizes given are with cases open. 1 in box.

F6544—Clouded pebbled ground, natural pink carnations and forget me not decorated, asstd. tinted Dresden pictures in gilt embossed frames, puffed crepe lining, 6 pcs., floral embossed beveled edge white back mirror and brush, white comb, manicure scissors, salve box, polisher, 9⅝x8⅛x6⅛............Each, **75c**

F6547—Natural asstd. color floral decorated dark ground covering, violet and leaf wreath bands on top with asstd. colored pictures in gold embossed frames, watered puffed mercerized lining, 6 pcs., bevel edge mirror, bristle brush, white celluloid comb, polisher, salve box and curved point nickel scissors, 10x8¼x6½........................Each, **$1.00**

F6548—Small dainty pink rose and leaf decorated peacock blue ground covering, bevel base, embossed edge, celluloid band round top over asstd. tinted pictures, watered puffed lining, 6 pcs., bevel edge mirror, bristle brush, white celluloid comb, polisher, salve box and curved point nickel scissors, 10x9¼x6¼....Each, **$1.22**

F6549½—Desk shape, shaded holly background, fancy beveled extension base, embossed edge celluloid top over asstd. "Winter Girl" pictures with wreath of holly and mistletoe, hand painted effect, mercerized puffed lining, 6 pcs., scroll and floral embossed bevel edge white back mirror and brush, comb, polisher, salve box and curved point manicure scissors, 10x9x7....Each, **$1.45**

F6551—Fancy shape, bevel base, rich clusters cherries and leaves on light ground, embossed edge celluloid top over colored juvenile group in cherry tree, extra quality puff lining, 6 pcs., bevel edge white back mirror and brush, comb, polisher, salve box and curved point manicure scissors. Each, **$1.75**

F6555—Extra quality large fittings, new artistic shape, full celluloid, large natural tinted bust figures with roses between, 2 bands of roses on top, under celluloid, double embossed gold trimmed borders, mahogany finish sides and base, embossed gold trimmed border, fine puffed satin lining, 9 pcs., hand painted and gold decorated large bevel edge mirror and extra good bristle brush, comb, white bone handle polisher, file, cuticle knife, powder and salve box, nickel curve point scissors, 13¾x15½x12½................Each, **$4.50**

F6547—Natural asstd. color floral decorated dark ground covering, violet and leaf wreath bands on top with asstd. colored pictures in gold embossed frames, watered puffed mercerized lining, 5 pcs., bevel edge mirror, bristle brush, white celluloid comb, polisher, salve box and curved point nickel scissors, 10x8¼x6¼....Each, **$1.00**

F6548—Small dainty pink rose and leaf decorated peacock blue ground covering, bevel base, embossed edge, celluloid band round top over asstd. flower girls, watered puffed lining, 5 pcs., bevel edge mirror, bristle brush, white celluloid comb, polisher, salve box and curved point nickel scissors, 10x9¼x6¼.....Each, **$1.22**

F6549—Rich large pink and yellow rose and leaf decorated moire effect gold and bronze green ground covering, celluloid top with dainty asstd. colored pictures in double embossed frames, mercerized puffed lining, 7 pcs., painted back bevel edge mirror and brush, comb, polisher, salve box, file and nickel scissors, 11¼x7¼x7¼.......... .....Each, **$1.42**

F6550—Rich floral decorated peacock blue ground covering, celluloid top and front, embossed edges over large American Beauty roses, bevel base, puffed mercerized lining, 5¼x4 mirror in roof, 6 pcs., painted back bevel edge hand mirror and bristle brush, comb, nail brush, polisher, salve box. 12⅝x10x6¾...........Each, **$1.75**

F6553—Extra good large fittings, asstd. medallion pictures under celluloid in gold metal beaded frame, figured silk plush edge top, tinted morning glory band around sides under double embossed celluloid, figured silk plush covered base, fine puffed satin lining, 10 pcs., gilt metal decorated back bevel edge mirror and brush, comb, bone handle polisher, file, cuticle knife, nickel scissors, powder and salve box, button hook, 10¾x12½x11.
Each, **$2.75**

F6554—*Biggest $5.00 value ever offered.* Asstd. colored medallion picture top with embossed bronze frame under celluloid, figured Savoy plush edges and sides, rich pink and white rose decorated moire effect gold ground covering, bevel base, puffed satin lining, gilt frame bevel edge mirror in roof mounted on figured plush mat with corded edges, 9 pcs., painted gold decorated back bevel edge mirror and brush, comb, powder and salve box, file, polisher, button hook, nickel scissors, 15⅛x13¾x9¼.......Each, **$3.15**

F6564—Green ground with asstd. floral decorations, bevel base, natural tinted bust figures on figured gold ground in front, wide gold trimmed embossed dark band edges under celluloid, moire puffed lining, hand painted gold trimmed back mirror and brush, comb, polisher, salve box, nickel scissors. 9⅝x9¼x8.....Each, **$1.85**

FANCY UPRIGHT CELLULOID TOILET AND MANICURE CASES—Contd.

F6562—Small variegated floral clusters on crystallized gold ground, asstd. tinted "Flower Girl" pictures under celluloid in embossed gold fram, figured plush front metal pull jewel drawer, puffed mercerized crepe lining, 7 pcs., hand painted mirror and brush, comb, file, polisher, salve box and bent point manicure scissors, 10½x13x 8½...... ....Each, **$1.42**

F6563—Special value. Rich floral decorated gold and dark ground covering, bevel extension base, embossed edge, celluloid top and front over asstd. landscape and sweetheart pictures in gold embossed frames, puffed mercerized cord trimmed lining, 6 pcs., mirror, brush, comb, polisher, salve box and nickel curved point manicure ....Each, **$1.72**

F6571—*Mammoth value.* Full celluloid and figured silk plush covered, red and pink rose and leaf decorated moire green ground covering, 10¼ x 6¾ top compartment on figured plush covered base with dainty natural tinted picture top, extra good large bristle painted back brush and hand mirror, 2 hexagon hinged front doors with tinted medallion pictures in embossed gold and green frames, double base, top with figured silk plush, 2 compartment jewel drawer with watch and ring holder, large gilt embossed drop pull handle, best puffed satin lining, silk cord trimmed, 7x2½ mirror in back of doors, 10¼x 7¼ mirror in back of center compartment holding 2 perfume bottles, large bone handle polisher, file, cuticle knife, curved point scissors, 20x14x18.................. .....Each, **$7.00**

F6569—Shaded red and white poppy decorated pebbled bronze green ground covering, figured silk plush covered sides and base, 9¼x4 celluloid covered compartment on top with medallion picture in embossed gold and green frame, double hinged doors in front with tinted medallion pictures in gold frames and embossed borders under celluloid, gilt pull celluloid front jewel drawer, extra good puffed satin lined throughout, silk cord trimmed, comb, painted back mirror and brush, polisher, 2 salve boxes, bone handle file, cuticle knife, button hook, nickel scissors, 19¼x10x13⅛.
Each, **$4.00**

FANCY UPRIGHT CELLULOID TOILET AND MANICURE CASES.

The best and most up to date line on the market. All with embossed gilt clasps and hinges, genuine bristle brushes and French plate bevel edge mirrors with gilt embossed and hand painted decorated backs except F6560. Sizes given are with cases open. 1 in box.

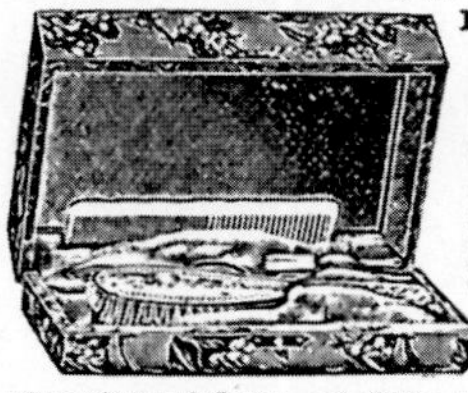

F6560—Natural color violet and leaf, gold trimmed decorated clouded pebble ground covering, asstd. colored pictures in embossed frame on top, bevel base, puffed mercerized lining, 8x5¼ mirror in roof, 5 pcs., bristle brush, white celluloid comb, combination bone handle file, nickel scissors, tweezers, 9¾x9x6½........Each, **75c**

F6561—Rich floral decorated clouded ground covering, asstd. medallion picture fronts in embossed gold frame, puffed lining, 8 pcs., mirror brush, comb, bone handle combination file, button hook, salve box, nickel scissors, 8½x10x7¼..........Each, **$1.10**

F6568—Heart shape, best quality figured silk plush and natural holly with berries under celluloid, embossed green, French red & gold traced bands on base, asstd. delicate tinted "Colonial Dame" in characteristic costumes with landscape scenes in heart shape frame, floral sprays under celluloid in gilt metal embossed frame, 2 embossed bands around side, fine quality puffed satin lining, 10 pcs., extra size hand painted mirror and brush, comb, polisher, scissors, file, knife, button hook, powder and salve boxes, 11½x13¾x12..........................Each, **$3.50**

F6567—Watered gold ground pink and blue natural color floral decorated covering, fancy waved front, 2 tinted medallion pictures on front and top in embossed frames under celluloid with embossed edges, puffed satin lining, silk cord trimmed, diamond shape mirror in roof, 5½x4½ mirror on doors, painted decorated back mirror and brush, comb, polisher, salve box, scissors, file, tweezers, button hook, 20¼x6¼x13..................Each, **$2.75**

F6565—*Exceptional value.* Fancy curved shape, bevel base, rich floral decorated moire gold and bronze green ground covering, dainty asstd. colored pictures on top and front, in gold and green embossed frames under celluloid with embossed edges, puffed satin lining, silk cord trimmed, 7 pcs., hand mirror, brush, comb, polisher, salve box, file, cuticle knife, 11x8¾x9¾. Each, **$2.00**

F6572—*Rare $12.00 value.* Gold moire ground, floral and blue bird dainty natural color decorated covering, figured silk plush sides, base and sub base, gold ornaments, top and double hinged front doors with tinted bust figures in embossed gold frames, gilt drop pull on jewel drawer with ring and watch holder, polisher, bone handle file, button hook, salve box in center compartment, 6x6 bevel edge mirror in back and round embossed gilt frame bevel edge mirrors on doors, hand mirror in roof, 2 perfume bottles, brush, comb and scissors, 24x13¼x18.

Each, **$7.75**

An Exceptionally Attractive Case, $3.79.

$3.79

No. 18K25156 This Case is exceptionally attractive. It is a number that not only contains good, useful articles but is very pretty and an exceptional value at our very low price of $3.79. This combination upright toilet case and manicure outfit has a very artistic shape, covered with fancy combination celluloid and figured plush; two pretty pictures on swinging doors in gilt frame; has a very beautifully decorated top; extension base covered with celluloid. This case is fitted with good quality highly decorated brush with bevel edge mirror to match, also a good quality white celluloid comb, with bone handled file, buttonhook, manicure scissors and chamois buffer. On inside of doors are two bevel edge mirrors in gilt frames. Satin lined throughout. Size, 10½x9½x6½ inches. Shipping weight, 5 pounds. Price, per set..... **$3.79**

F6566—Fancy curved top and extension base, delicately tinted pink roses with leaves on dark ground, colonial lads and lasses in bright costumes on moire gold ground with floral sprays under embossed gold & green edged celluloid, metal pull celluloid front jewel or trinket drawer, 9 pcs., hand decorated white back mirror and brush, comb, scissors, etc., 2 bevel edge mirrors in back of doors, mercerized puffed twilled lining. 18x8¼x12½..Each, **$2.50**

Celluloid Toilet Cases. Exceptional Values.

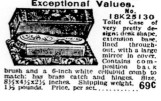

No. 18K25130 Toilet Case of very pretty design; desk shape, extension base, lined throughout, with a large mirror in cover. Contains composition back brush and a 6-inch white celluloid comb to match; has brass catch and hinges. Size, 8½x4½x2½ inches. Shipping weight, 1½ pounds. Price, per set........... **69c**

CELLULOID TOILET CASES.

Better values and more artistic shapes and coverings than ever. Carefully selected from the leading manufacturers. All with genuine bristle brushes and hand mirrors. Brush with fancy scroll and floral embossed backs. Each with gilt clasp and hinges. Sizes are given with cases open. Each in box.

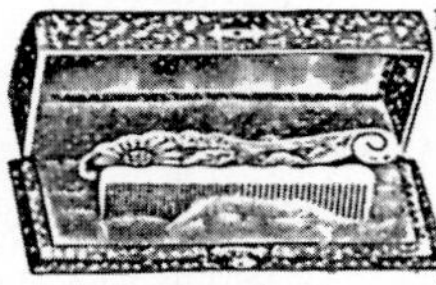

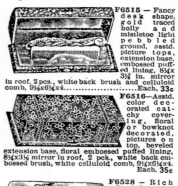

F6515—Fancy desk shape, gold traced holly and mistletoe light pebbled ground, asstd. picture tops, extension base, embossed puffed lining, 8¼x3½ in. mirror in roof, 2 pcs., white back brush and celluloid comb, 9½x6¼x4......................Each, **33c**

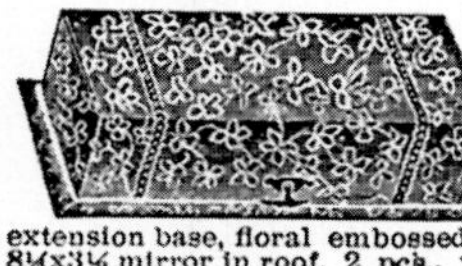

F6516—Asstd. color decorated catchy covering, floral or bowknot decorated, pictures on top, beveled extension base, floral embossed puffed lining, 8¼x3½ mirror in roof, 2 pcs., white back embossed brush, white celluloid comb, 9¼x6¼x4. Each, **35c**

F6528—Rich floral decorated gold and bronze green ground, celluloid top over asstd. floral bouquet and miniature effects, puffed mercerized lining, 3 pcs., beveled edge floral white back hand mirror and brush, white celluloid comb, 8¾x7x6¾..........Each, **$1.00**

F6529—Full celluloid covered, exquisite natural chrysanthemums, hand painted effect, green clouded ground, embossed bronze green gold traced bands, rich green tinted mission oak ends, embossed scroll beveled base, 3 pcs., floral embossed gold traced white back mirror and brush, white celluloid comb, fine mercerized puffed lining, 10x6½x4¾.......Each, **$1.05**

F6526—Beautiful bronze, green & gold moire ground, small pink roses with leaves covering, extension plush covered base, celluloid top over asstd. dresden pictures puffed crepe lining, 3 pcs., beveled edge white back mirror and brush, celluloid comb. Each. **92c**

F6527—Natural holly and mistletoe decorated clouded gr'nd covering, beveled extension base, "Winter Scene" landscape with pine branch wreath under embossed edge celluloid top, mercerized puffed lining, beveled edge floral embossed white back mirror and brush, white celluloid comb.............Each, **98c**

No. 18K25143 Special Value Combination Toilet and Manicure Set in plush and celluloid case. Top of case is decorated with very pretty miniature under transparent celluloid, with gilt embossed edges; has extension base of mottled plush and floral decorations on side and inside of cover. Sateen lined throughout; brass catch and hinges, composition back brush highly decorated in colors with bevel edge mirror to match, salve jar, bone nail file, bone handled buttonhook and chamois buffer, also a 5¾-inch celluloid comb. Size, 11x9x3 inches. Shipping weight, 2½ pounds. This case is a regular $3.50 value. Price, per set. **$2.19**

FANCY CELLULOID MANICURE SETS—Cont'd

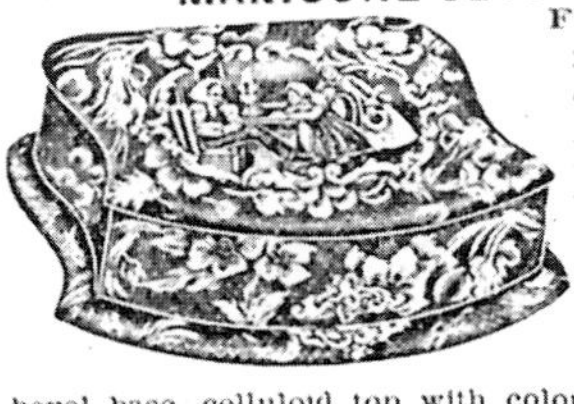

F6585—Asstd. natural color rich red and white poppy decorated silver and bronze green ground covering, figured plush bevel base, celluloid top with colored asstd. medallion pictures in embossed gilt frames, cord trimmed, puffed satin lining, 7 fittings, powder and salve box, scissors, large bone handle polisher, cuticle knife, file and tweezers, 11x11x8¾..... ... .Set, **$1.75**

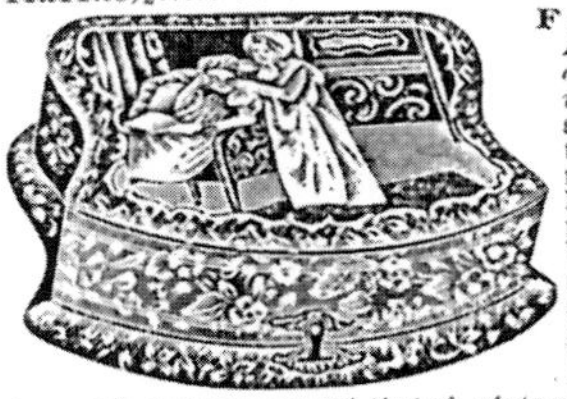

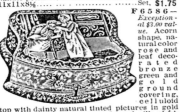

F6586—*Exception-al $3.00 value.* Acorn shape, natural color rose and leaf decorated bronze green and gold ground covering, celluloid top with dainty natural tinted pictures in gold and green embossed frames, figured silk plush base, silk cord trimmed puffed satin lining, 8 extra good fittings, powder and salve box, scissors, fancy bone handle polisher, cuticle knife, file, tweezers, button hook, 10x12x9¼.
Set, **$2.00**

FANCY CELLULOID MANICURE SETS.

All with embossed gilt metal clasps and hinges, fittings on spring holders. Sizes given are with cases open. Each in box.

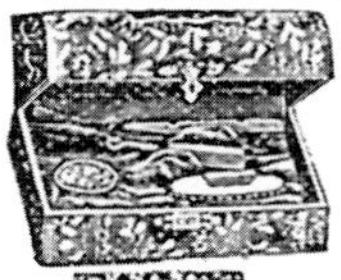

F6578—Dainty clouded ground, natural floral decorated covering, fancy top, extension base, puffed sateen lined, 4 fittings, polisher, file, salve box and scissors, 6½x6x4¾.
Set, **35c**

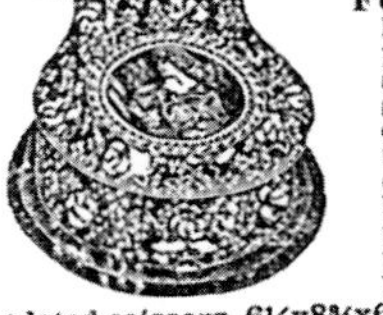

F6579½—"Good Luck" horseshoe shape, bevel plush covered extension base, pebbled ground, rich natural color floral decorated, tinted pictures under celluloid in gilt embossed frame, puffed mercerized lining, 4 pcs., polisher, salve box, file and nickel plated scissors, 6½x8¾x6¼............Set, **50c**

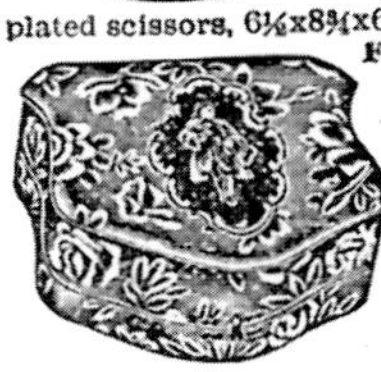

F6581—Artistic shape, extension base, rich red cherry and blossom decorated bronze green ground, tinted juvenile pictures in gilt frame, celluloid embossed edge top, mercerized puffed crepe lining, 5 pcs., polisher, salve box, file, manicure scissors and button hook, 6¾x9¼x6¾.........................Set, **72c**

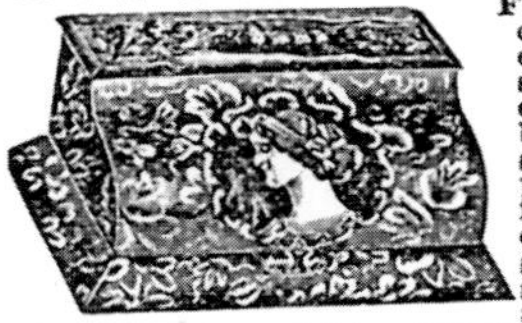

F6584—Full celluloid covered, desk shape, bevel extension base, variegated sweet peas with foliage decorated clouded green ground, asstd. landscape and dainty miniature effects in embossed gold frames, fine quality puffed satin lining, 6 large pcs., polisher, salve box, file, button hook, knife and scissors, 8¾x8¾x6¼........Set, **$1.50**

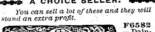

A CHOICE SELLER.

You can sell a lot of these and they will stand an extra profit.

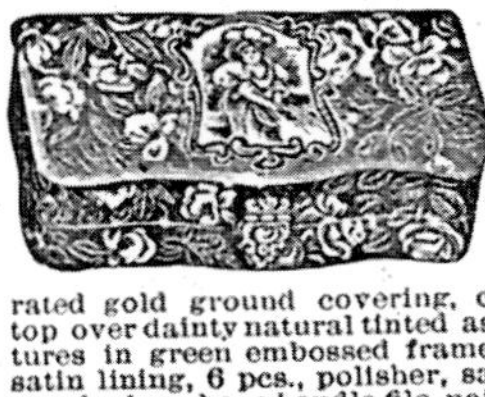

F6582—Dainty natural color mall pink rose and leaf decorated gold ground covering, celluloid top over dainty natural tinted asstd. pictures in green embossed frame, puffed satin lining, 6 pcs., polisher, salve and powder box, bone handle file, nail brush, scissors, 9¼x6¾x6¾.
Per set, **$1.00**

FANCY CELLULOID MANICURE SETS.

All with embossed gilt metal clasps and hinges, fittings on spring holders. New and fancy shapes. Sizes given are with cases open. 1 in box.

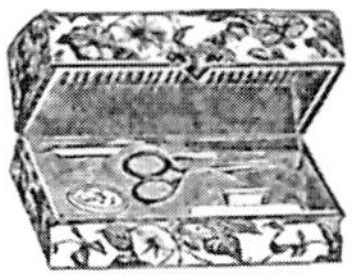

F6578

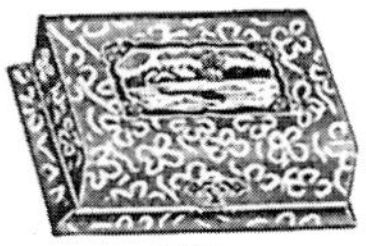

F6579

F6578—Dainty natural color asstd. morning glory decorated covering, gilt embossed frame medallion picture on top, puffed twilled lining, 4 pcs., polisher, salve box, file, scissors, 6x6¾x4¾...... ....Set, **35c**

F6579—Fancy embossed bow knot design asstd. pink, blue and red covering, colored medallion picture in embossed gilt frame on top, bevel base, puffed lining, 5 pcs., polisher, salve box, file, button hook, scissors, 6¾x6¾x5...... ....Set, **50c**

SATIN FINISH CELLULOID COLLAR AND CUFF BOXES.

All with beautiful hand painted natural color floral decorations on tops and sides, silk ribbon bows and hinges, asstd. colors. 1 in box.

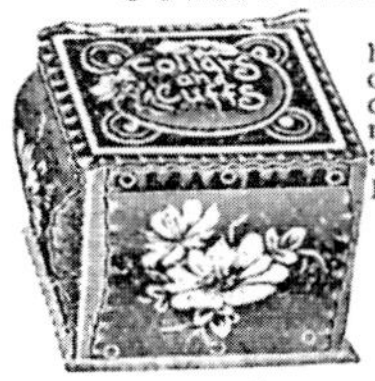

F6232—Asstd. colors, crimped gold edges, embossed cover, gold lettering "Collars and Cuffs," neatly lined, 6½x6¾x5.
Each, 37c

F6233—Asstd. pink and blue satin finish, swell sides with 4 laced ribbon bow corners, crimped edge top neatly decorated and lettered "Collars and Cuffs," embossed lining, 7¾x7¾x5½. Each, **65c**

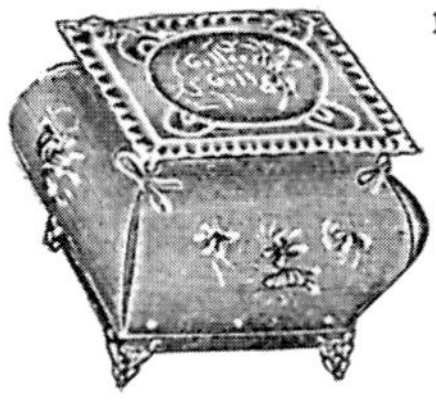

F6234—New and odd shape, satin finish, asstd. colors, 4 brass metal feet, 4 ribbon bow laced corners, embossed and crimped gold edge floral decorated and lettered "Collars and Cuffs," ribb'n hinged top. 7½x 7½x6½.
Each, **72c**

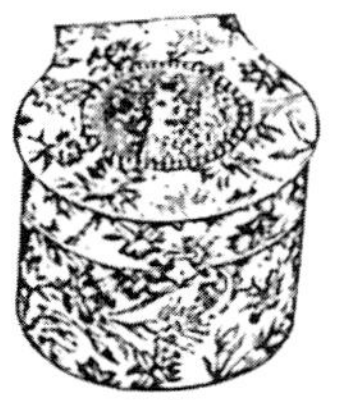

F6421

F6421—Horseshoe shape, asstd. floral decorated dark ground, colored medallion picture under celluloid, embossed frame, puffed lined lid, 5¾x7¾x9¾.
Each, **32c**

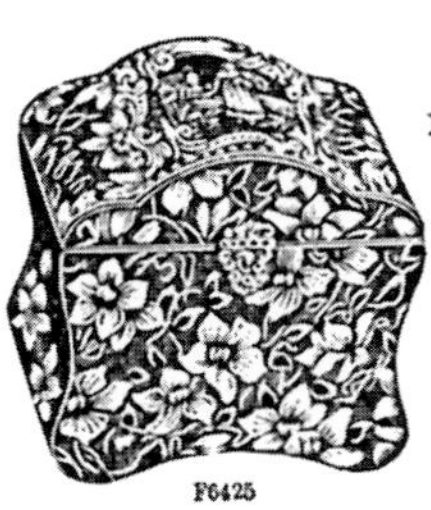

F6425

F6425—Gold moire effect ground, asstd. pink and blue clematis decorated covering, celluloid top over natural tinted medallion pictures in embossed bronze frame, mercerized crepe puffed lining, 7½ x8x11¼.
Each, **69c**

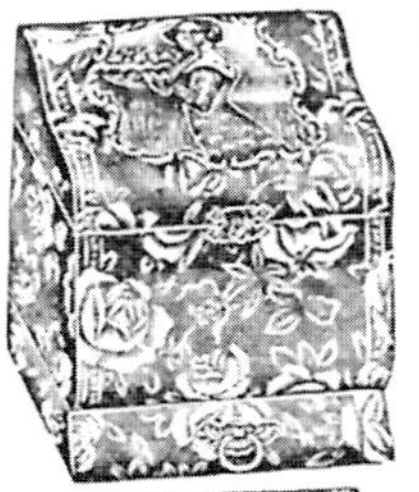

F6428—Watered gold and green bronze ground, pink and yellow rose decorated covering, embossed edge, celluloid top and front, asstd. medallion pictures in embossed gold frame, jewel or button drawer, embossed gilt pull, puffed satin lined drawer and lid, 6½x10½x12.
Each, **$1.00**

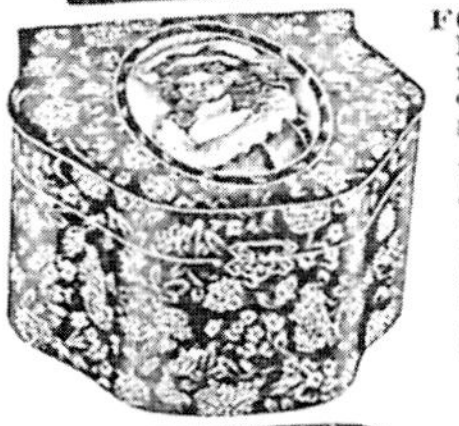

F6429—Full celluloid over asstd. rich carnation decorated gold ground covering, 2 embossed bands round side, extension cover with asstd. picture medallions in gold scroll embossed frame, puffed satin lining, 8¼x8¾x11⅜.
Each. **$1.20**

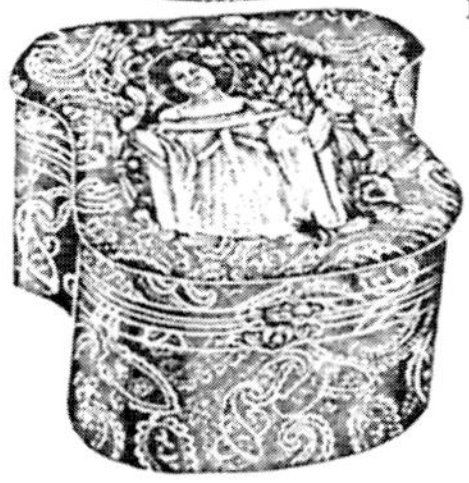

F6430—Acorn shape, full celluloid under new and artistic oriental effect bronze green and gold ground covering, cover with asstd. tinted flower girls in gold embossed frame, puffed satin lined, extra compartment for buttons, etc., 9x 10x12½.
Each, **$1.39**

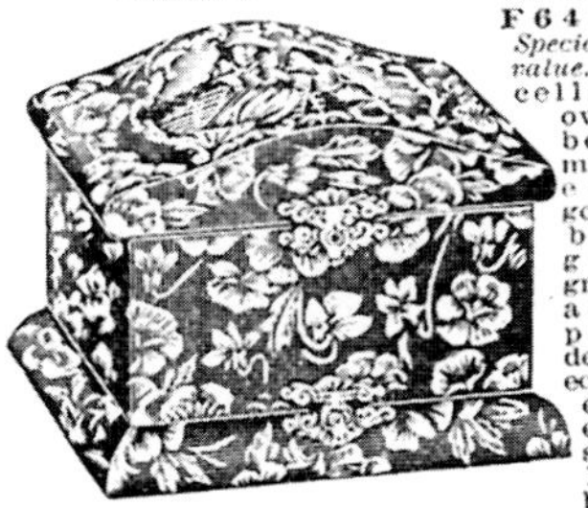

F6431—*Special $3.00 value.* Full celluloid overembossed moire effect gold and bronze green ground, asstd. pansy decorated covering, extension lid and base, asstd. tinted geisha girls in bronze green and gold frame, extra good puffed satin lining, embossed gold button holder in top, separate hdkf. compartment in bottom, 9¾x10x12¾. Ea. **$1.75**

SPECIAL VALUE COLLAR AND CUFF BOX.

FOR A DOLLAR leader will show up well along side others at $1.50.

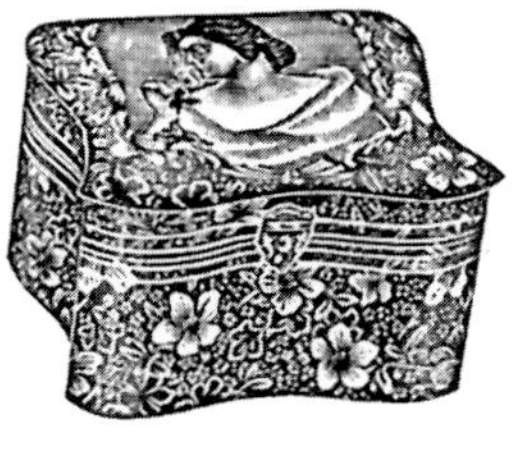

F6426—Fancy shape, moire effect bronze green and gold ground, large pink and white rose decorated covering, celluloid top, asstd. tinted pictures in embossed floral and rope effect frame, satin puffed lining, 8¾x9x11⅝.
Each, **72c**

FANCY CELLULOID COLLAR AND CUFF BOXES.

New and up to date goods selected from the leading manufacturers. The best line shown in America. Each with gilt metal clasp. Sizes given are with boxes open. 1 in box except F6420.

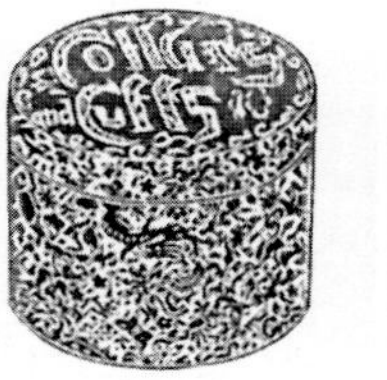

F6420

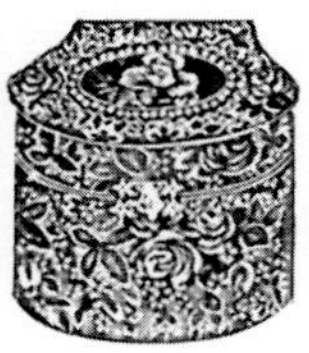

F6421

F6420—*A 25 cent leader.* Fancy floral asstd. colored decorated covering, celluloid embossed "Collars and Cuffs" top with floral scroll design, 6¼x5. 3 in box.... Each, **18c**

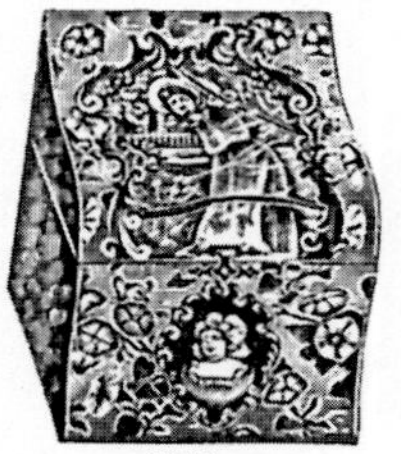

F6422

F6421—Horseshoe shape, large red rose and floral decorated covering, tinted bust figure picture under celluloid in embossed gilt frames, puffed lining, 6x7¾x9¾. Each, **32c**

F6422—Dainty asstd. colored morning glory decorated covering, asstd. pictures on top and front in embossed gold frame, puffed lining in lid, 6x8½x10. Each, **37c**

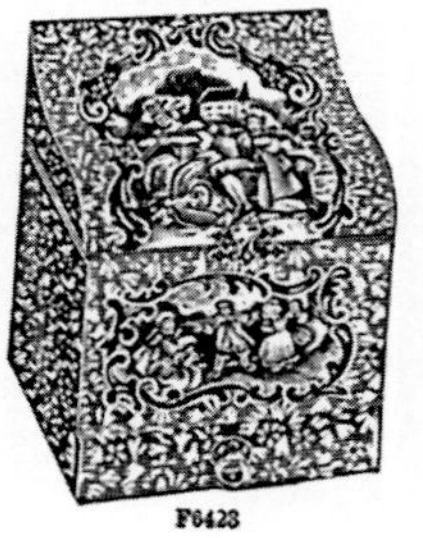

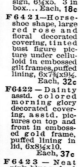

F6423

F6423—Neat pink, blue and red floral decorated gold ground covering, asstd. tinted pictures on top and front in embossed gold trimmed frame, button or jewel drawer in bottom with gilt ring pull, puffed mercerized lined lid, 6⅛x8⅛x11¼. Each, **50c**

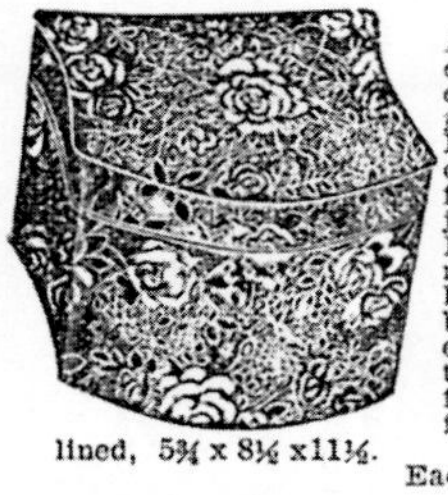

F6428½—*Extra quality on which you can double your money.* Full celluloid over beautifully tinted jack, tea and La France roses with leaves and buds on clouded green gold traced ground, fine quality full satin lined, 5¾ x 8¼ x11¼. Each, **$1.00**

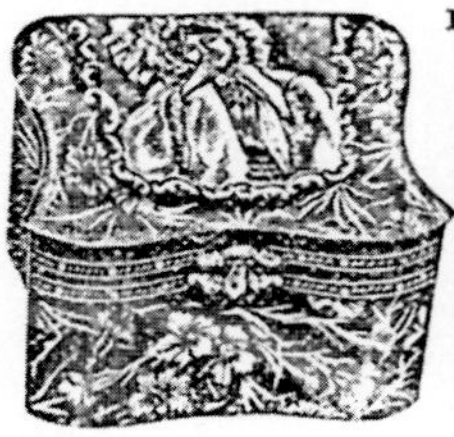

F6429½—Full celluloid top and front over daintily tinted pictures, variegated sweet peas on shaded moire effect ground, gilt metal pull hdkf. or button drawer bototm, extension base, puffed satin lined lid and drawer, 8x9¾x12¼. Each, **$1.25**

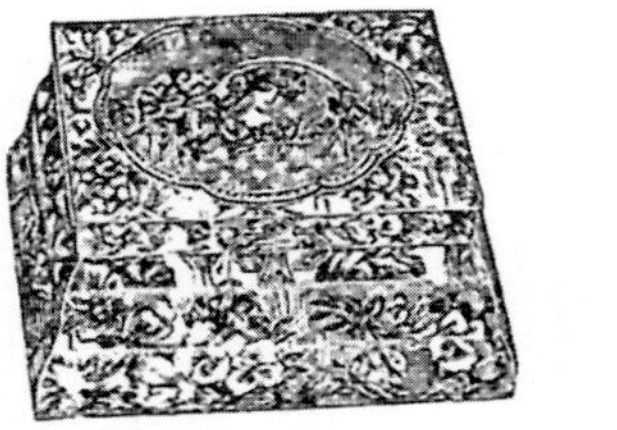

F6431—*Special $3.00 value.* Full celluloid covered, fancy curved sides, heavy embossed band around bottom, pansy bouquets in contrasting shades on silver birch ground covering, asstd. beautifully tinted miniature picture tops, in gold embossed frames, full lined best quality puffed satin, 4⅝x9¼x10¾. Each, **$1.75**

FANCY CELLULOID SMOKERS' SETS.

The best values carefully selected from the principal manufacturers. Each with gilt clasp and hinges, all puffed lined. 1 in box. Sizes given are with cases open.

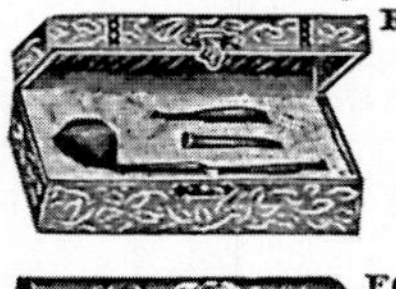

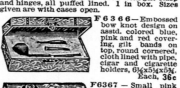

F6366—Embossed bow knot design on asstd. colored blue, pink and red covering, gilt bands on top, round cornered, cloth lined with pipe, cigar and cigarette holders, 6⅛x5¼x5¾. Each, **36c**

F6367 — Small pink and red rose decorated bronze green ground covering, medallion picture top, mercerized crepe lining, 4 pcs., briar pipe, cigar and cigarette holders, engraved nickel match safe, 7x7x6........................... Each, **50c**

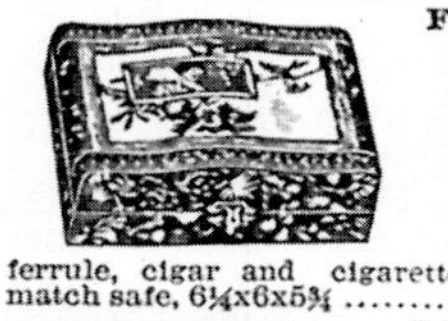

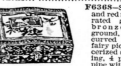

F6368—Small pink and red rose, decorated gold and bronze green ground, fancy curved top with fairy picture, mercerized sateen lining, 4 pcs., briar pipe with sterling ferrule, cigar and cigarette holders, nickel match safe, 6¼x6x5¾ .... Each, **67c**

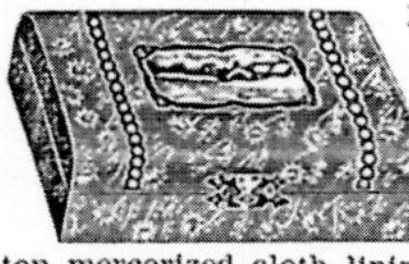

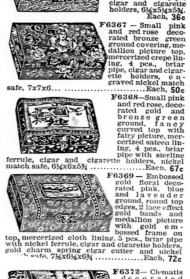

F6369— Embossed gold floral decorated pink, blue and lavender ground, round top edges, 2 lace effect gold bands and medallion picture with gold embossed frame on top, mercerized cloth lining, 5 pcs., briar pipe with nickel ferrule, cigar and cigarette holders, gold charm spring cigar cutter and nickel match safe, 7½x6½x6¾ .... Each, **72c**

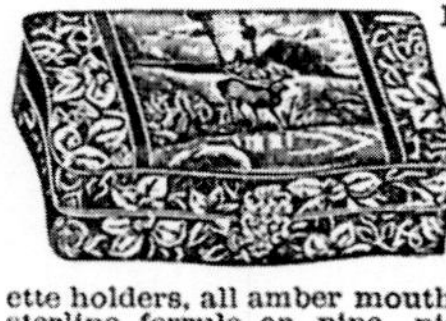

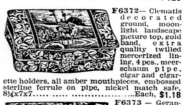

F6372— Clematis decorated ground, moonlight landscape picture top, gold band, extra quality twilled mercerized lining, 4 pcs., meerschaum pipe, cigar and cigarette holders, all amber mouthpieces, embossed sterling ferrule on pipe, nickel match safe, 8¼x7x7 ....Each, **$1.18**

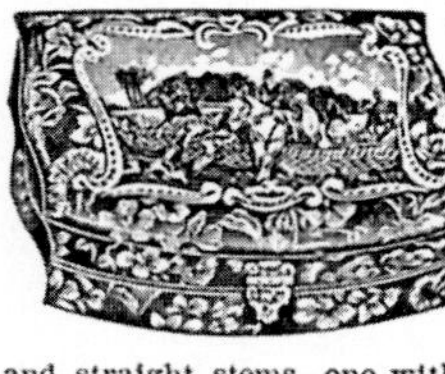

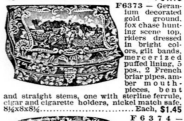

F6373 — Geranium decorated gold ground, fox chase hunting scene top, riders dressed in bright colors, gilt bands, mercerized puffed lining, 5 pcs., 2 French briar pipes, amber mouthpieces, bent and straight stems, one with sterling ferrule, cigar and cigarette holders, nickel match safe, 8¼x8x8¾.............................Each, **$1.45**

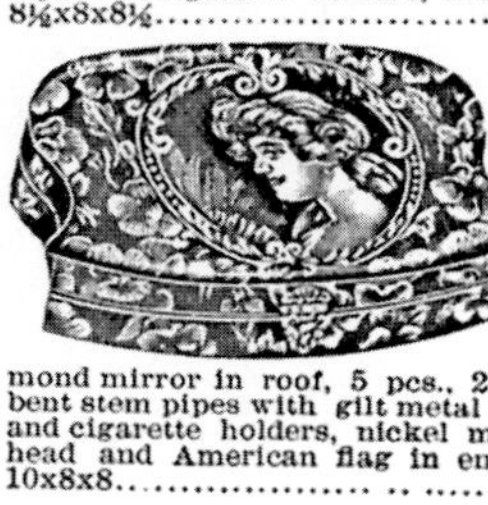

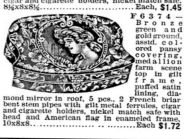

F6374 — Bronze green and gold ground, asstd. colored pansy covering, medallion farm scene top in gilt frame, puffed satin lining, diamond mirror in roof, 5 pcs., 2 French briar bent stem pipes with gilt metal ferrules, cigar and cigarette holders, nickel match safe with head and American flag in enameled frame, 10x8x8.................. .. ..Each **$1.72**

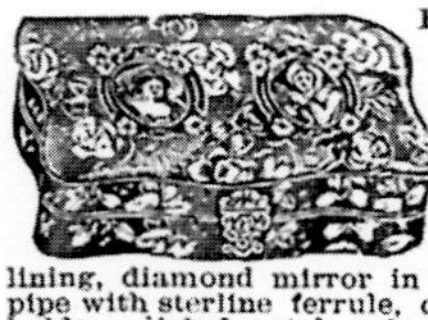

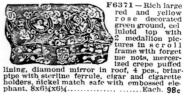

F6371 — Rich large red and yellow rose decorated green ground, celluloid top with 2 medallion pictures in scroll frame with forget me nots, mercerized crepe puffed lining, diamond mirror in roof, 4 pcs., briar pipe with sterling ferrule, cigar and cigarette holders, nickel match safe with embossed elephant, 8x6¼x6¼.............. ....Each, **98c**

CELLULOID INFANTS' SETS.

Gilt clasps and hinges, puffed lining. Sizes given are with cases open. 1 set in box.

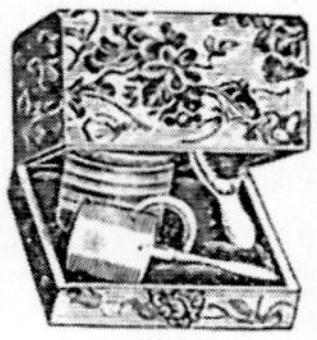

F6510

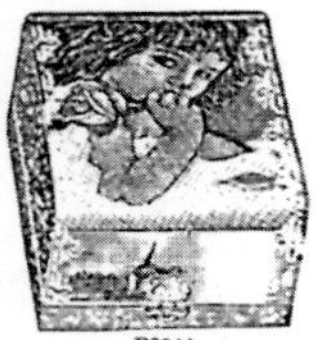

F6511

F6510—Natural color violet and leaf decorated covering, mercerized lining, 4 pcs.—celluloid comb, bone teething ring, soft bristle bone handle brush, embossed metal powder box—5x9x7.................................. Set, **75c**

F6511—Small red and pink rose and leaf decorated covering, embossed edge full celluloid top over asstd. colored pictures, mercerized twilled lining, 4 pcs.—bone teething ring, soft bristle brush, white celluloid comb, embossed metal powder box—5x9x7. Set, **98c**

CELLULOID INFANTS' SETS.

Gilt clasps and hinges, puffed lining. Sizes given are with cases open. Each set in box.

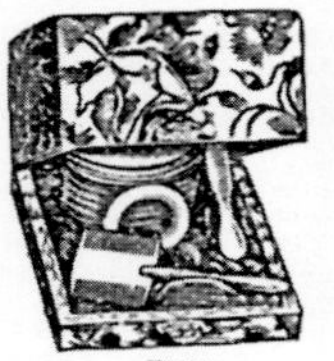

F6510

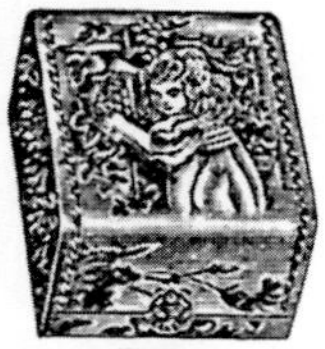

F6511

F6510—Dainty pansy decorated light ground, medallion picture tops, embossed frame, puffed mercerized lining, 4 pcs., celluloid comb, bone handle soft bristle brush and teething ring, embossed metal powder box, 5x9x7............................ ....Set, **75c**

F6511—Asstd. natural color floral & leaf decorated light ground covering, embossed edge celluloid top over dainty juvenile medallions, good quality puffed mercerized lining, 4 pcs., embossed metal powder box, soft bristle wire drawn bone handle brush, celluloid comb and teething ring, 5x9x7. Set, **98c**

CELLULOID POST CARD OR PHOTO HOLDERS.

Extraordinary values. New shapes. 1 in box.

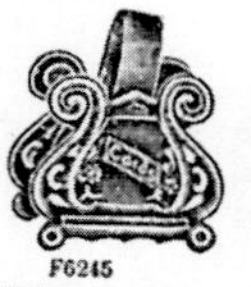

F6245

F2646

F6245—Special 25c card basket. Asstd shapes and colors, gilt crimped edges, neatly lined. 6x2¼. Each, **17c**

F6247

F6246—Asstd. pink and blue, satin finish, transparent red celluloid embossed crimped gold trimmed sides hand painted poppy decorated, embossed puffed lined bottom. 7x7¼x3. Each, **34c**

F6247—2 compartment, embossed gold crimped edge, asstd. pink and blue satin finish and transparent red celluloid embossed with tinted art nouveau picture fronts. 7¼ x6¼x3..Each, **36c**

FANCY CELLULOID SHAVING SETS—Cont'd

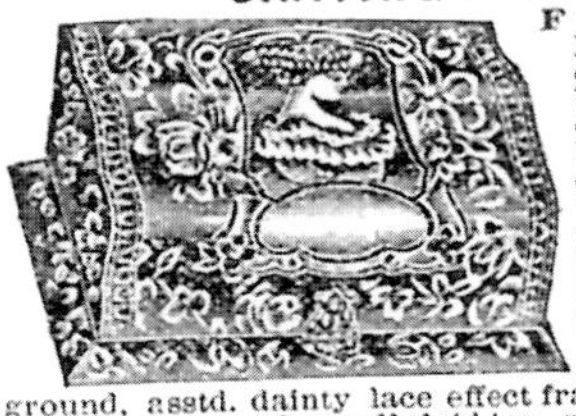

F6387—Fancy curved top, beveled extension base, delicate pink, white and red primroses with foliage on moire bronze green ground, asstd. dainty lace effect frame picture tops, embossed edge, celluloid top, puffed satin lining, bone handle bristle brush, scalloped edge floral decorated china partition mug, 4 in. round beveled ring handle mirror, 9¾x10¼x7¼. Each, **$1.45**

DESK SHAPE.

An extremely popular and profitable seller.

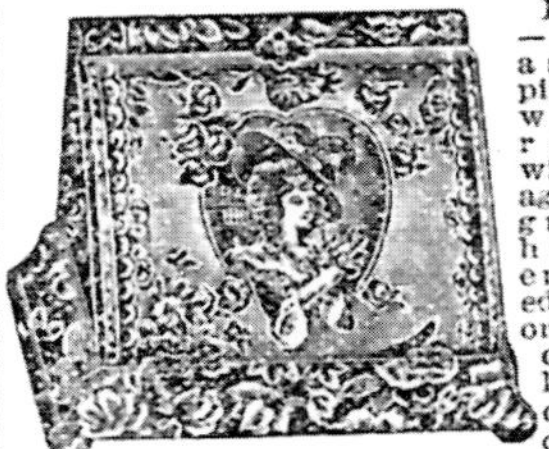

F6388—Rich asstd. pink and white roses with foliage, dark ground, heavy embossed 3 color edge, celluloid top over dainty tinted medallion "Court Dames," heart design, roses and violet sprays, puffed moire lining. 5 pieces, bristle brush, gold edge floral decorated china mug, 4 in. round beveled ring handle mirror, manicure scissors and Sheffield razor, 9¼x6¾. Each, **$1.75**

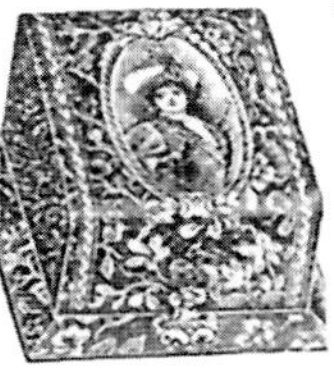

F6381—Dainty cherry blossoms on bronze green moire ground, asstd. medallion head picture tops under celluloid, embossed edges, mercerized puffed lining, white handle bristle brush, partition mug, floral decorated, gold showered edge and handle, 6⅛x10x6¾. Each, **67c**

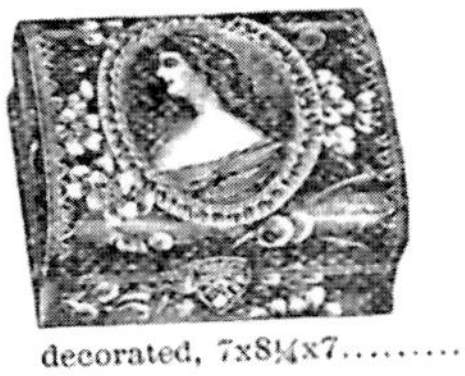

F6383½—Asstd. natural tinted medallion heads in embossed bronze frame under celluloid, rich shaded wild rose on gold moire ground, puffed mercerized lining, bristle brush, embossed gold edge partition mug, floral decorated, 7x8¼x7. Each, **73c**

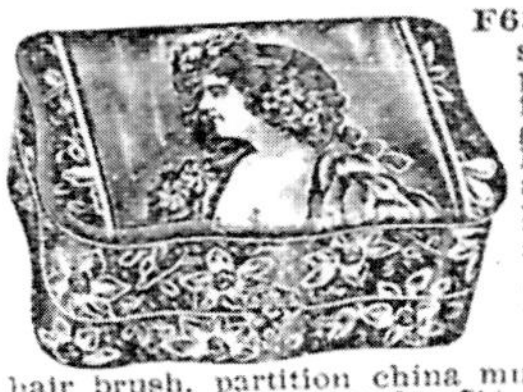

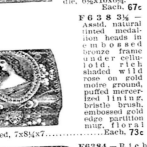

F6384—Rich shaded red poppies with foliage on gilt ground, celluloid top with asstd. tinted medallion heads, bronze bands, puffed mercerized lining, white handle badger hair brush, partition china mug, floral decorated, razor holder, 8⅞x8¾x7¼. Each, **84c**

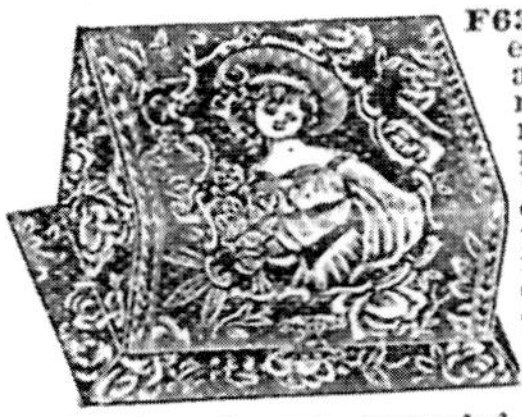

F6385—Beveled extension base, asstd. large natural pink, red and tea roses, foliage background, dainty asstd. picture tops in rich colors under celluloid, 2 embossed gold bands, extra good mercerized lining, 5¾x7 mirror in top, enameled handle bristle brush, embossed scalloped edge, floral decorated china partition mug, 6½x10½x6¾. Each, **95c**

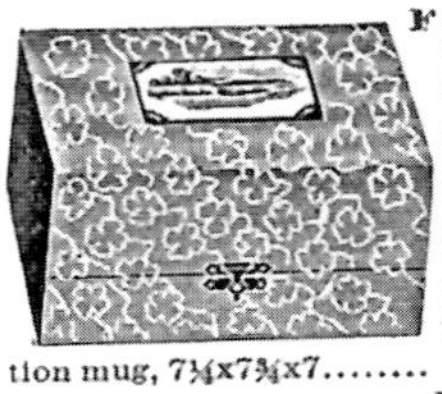

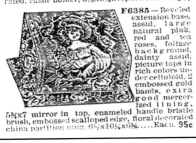

F6379—Embossed bow knot design on asstd. colored pink, blue and red ground covering, landscape picture top in gold embossed frame, puffed cloth lining, 5x7 mirror in roof, black enamel handle bristle brush, gold showered edge floral decorated partition mug, 7¼x7¾x7. Each, **37c**

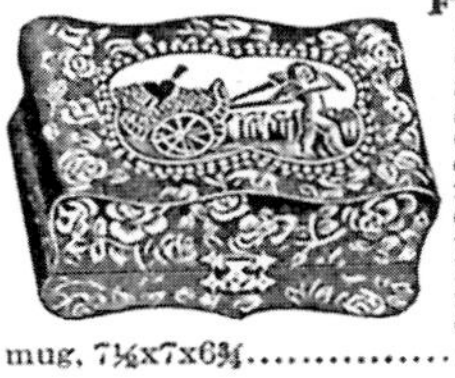

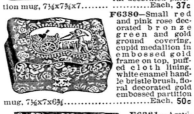

F6380—Small red and pink rose decorated bronze green and gold ground covering, cupid medallion in embossed gold frame on top, puffed cloth lining, white enamel handle bristle brush, floral decorated gold embossed partition mug, 7½x7x6¾. Each, **50c**

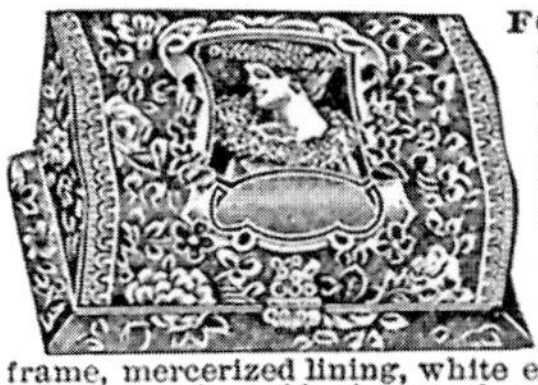

F6381—Asstd. colored pink, blue and lavender floral decorated gold moire effect ground covering, embossed edge, celluloid top with medallion in embossed gold frame, mercerized lining, white enamel handle bristle brush, gold showered embossed edge floral decorated partition mug, 6⅛x10x7. Each, **67c**

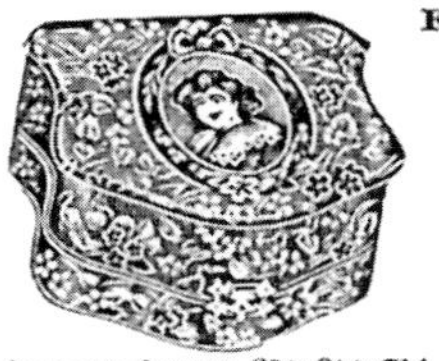

F6382—Asstd. floral decorated embossed asstd. colored ground coverings, celluloid top with bouquet in embossed gold frame, extra good twilled puffed lining, white enamel handle bristle brush, gold sponged handle and edge floral decorated mug, 6¾x8½x7½. Each, **72c**

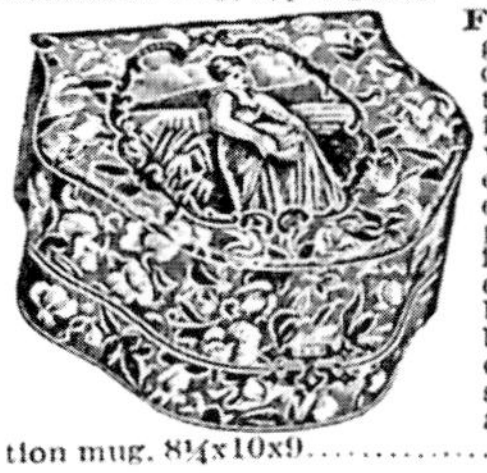

F6383—Pebbled ground sweet pea decorated gold trimmed covering, celluloid top with picture in embossed frame, extra quality puffed mercerized lining, white enamel handle bristle brush, embossed floral decorated gold sponged handle and edge partition mug, 8¼x10x9. Each, **75c**

WHISK BROOM HOLDERS.

Exceptional values. Odd and fancy shapes.

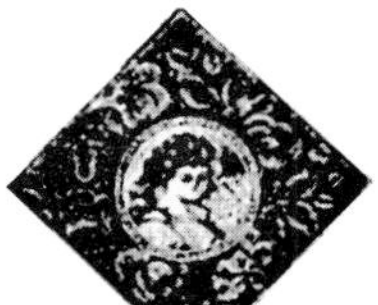

F6614 F6615

F6614—Asstd. colored figured plush covered, medallion picture in gilt embossed frame under celluloid, pocket back, metal hanger, 8x8. 3 in box. Each, **17c**

F6615—*Exceptional 25 cent value.* Japanese fancy straw woven backs with twist edges and hanger, hand painted floral decorated, ribbon bow tied, celluloid holder, average 7x8¼. 6 shapes in box asstd. Each, **18c**

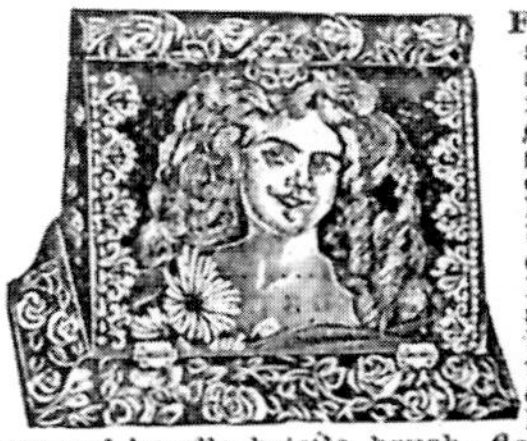

F6388—Desk shape, rich small pink rose and leaf decorated gold ground covering, heavily embossed 3 color edge, celluloid top over asstd. colored bouquets, extra good mercerized puffed lining, white enamel handle bristle brush, floral decorated embossed mug, 4 in. white back bevel edge ring handled mirror, extra good Sheffield razor and manicure scissors, 9¾x11x6¾. Each, **$1.75**

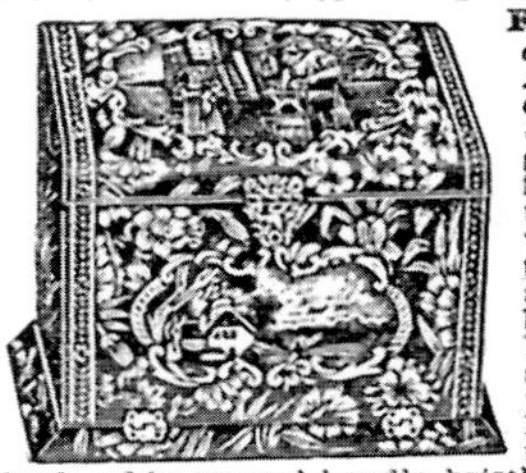

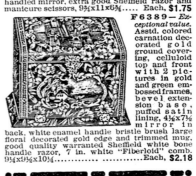

F6389—*Exceptional value.* Asstd. colored carnation decorated gold ground covering, celluloid top and front with 2 pictures in gold and green embossed frames, bevel extension base, puffed satin lining, 4⅛x7½ mirror in back, white enamel handle bristle brush large floral decorated gold edge and trimmed mug, good quality warranted Sheffield white bone handle razor, 7 in. white "Fiberloid" comb, 9¼x9½x10¼. Each, **$2.18**

$5.00 SHAVING SET.

NOWHERE ELSE can you get as good a one to retail for the money.

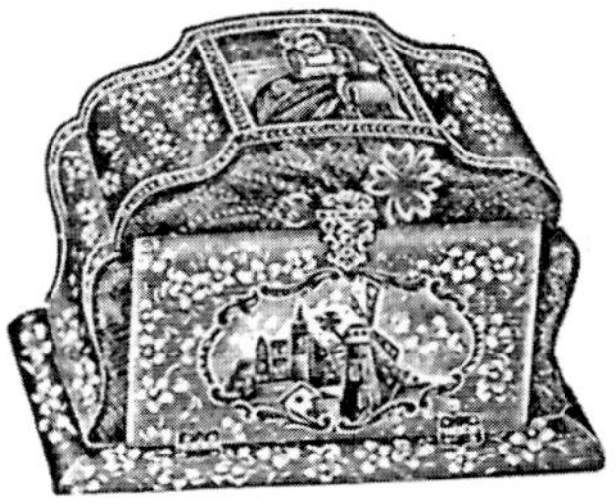

F6390—Seal grain silver and bronze green ground covering with asstd. pink and red poppies and foliage, full celluloid cover, 2 beautiful colored medallion pictures on front and top in embossed frames, figured silk plush trim front and back edges, puffed satin lining, white bone handle bristle brush, embossed and floral decorated partition mug, 4x5¼ bevel edge white back ring handle mirror, warranted hollow ground magnetic steel razor with white bone handle, curved point nickel manicure scissors, 7 in. white "Fiberloid" comb, 10⅝x11x11. Each, **$3.00**

WHISK BROOM HOLDERS.

Positively the best sellers on the market. Odd and fancy shapes.

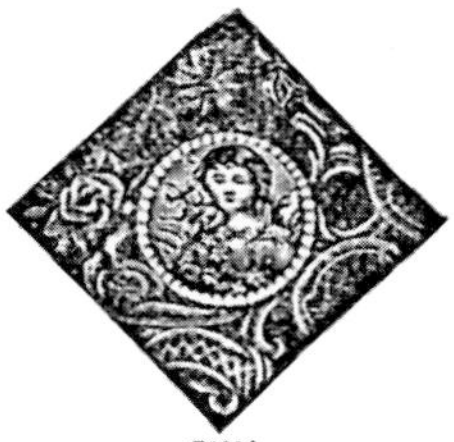

F6614

F6614—Asstd. colored figured plush covered, medallion picture in gilt embossed frame under celluloid, pocket back, metal hanger, 8x8. 3 in box. Each, **17c**

FANCY CELLULOID
WORK BOXES.

New and fancy shapes, all with bone handle fittings, puffed linings, gilt embossed clasps and hinges. Sizes given are with cases open. Each in box.

F6600—Floral decorated bronze-green ground, asstd. dainty medallion pictures, puffed mercerized lining, 5 pcs. in holders on bar, 6¼x5¾x6⅛. ......Each, **36c**

F6601—Tinted asstd. pink, blue and lavender floral decorated, light pebbled ground, celluloid top over natural tinted pictures in gilt and floral frames, 6x4¾ mirror in roof, mercerized lining, 5 pcs. in holders on bar, 6½x6¼ x7¼.........Each, **50c**

F6603—Celluloid top over wide panel landscape scene and floral spray, gold band outlining, large pink and white carnations on light pebbled ground, puffed mercerized lining, diamond shape mirror in roof, 6 pcs. in holders on bar, 8¾x7x7½... ..Each, **73c**

F6604—Dainty violet decorated bronze green ground, embossed green trimmed celluloid top over natural tinted pictures, diamond mirror in roof, mercerized twilled lining, 6 pcs. on hinged bar holder, 9x7¾x7¾.
.....Each, **$1.00**

F6279—Wood frame box, daisy floral design on asstd. color grounds covering, asstd. pictures under transparent celluloid, gilt embossed borders, hinged cover, diamond shape mirror, puff lining in roof, removable compartment tray, padded pin cushion, 5 piece fittings including scissors, 6¾x5x3¼. 1 in box. Each, **35c**

FANCY CELLULOID
WORK BOXES.

New and fancy shapes, all with bone handle fittings, puffed linings, gilt embossed clasps and hinges. Sizes given are with cases open. 1 in box.

F6600—Natural color floral decorated, embossed gilt frame, floral trimmed medallion picture on top, mercerized lining, 4 pcs. in holders on bar, 6¾x6¼x 7¼.......Each, **36c**

F6279—Wood frame box, red, green and tan embossed Mexican carved leather effect, asstd. colored pictures under transparent celluloid gilt metal corners, lock and key, puff lining, diamond shape mirror, 5 piece fittings, including scissors, 2 pin cushions, 6¾x4¾x 3. 1 in box. Each, **33c**

F6279

F6605—Rich floral and blue bird decorated gold ground, celluloid top over asstd. medallion pictures in double gilt frame, gilt metal frame mirror in roof, satin lining, 6 pcs. on floral embossed plush cover hinged bar holder, 9¾x9x9¾. ....Each, **$1.20**

F6606—Rare $2.00 value. Red geranium and leaf decorated gold and bronze green ground, silk plush embossed bands celluloid top over dainty tinted pictures in gilt frame, gilt metal frame diamond mirror in roof, satin lining, 8 pcs. on hinged bar holder, 10½x10x9¾.....Each, **$1.42**

F6607—Rich floral decorated gold ground, full celluloid, asstd. medallion pictures on top in gilt and green trimmed embossed frame, 2 compartments, jewel drawer with watch and ring holder, gilt metal pull, satin lined throughout, 7 pcs. on hinged bar holder, 10x9¾x10 ..Each, **$1.75**

F6605—Rich asstd. floral and blue bird decorated gold ground, celluloid top over asstd. medallion pictures in double gilt frame, gilt metal frame mirror in roof, satin lining, 6 pcs. on floral embossed plush cover hinged bar holder, 9¾x9x9¾. ......Each, **$1.20**

F6607½—Fancy shape, curved top, full celluloid covered, variegated pink and red carnations with foliage decorated green ground, pastoral scenes in embossed gold scroll frame, gilt ring pull jewel drawer, 2 compartments, watch and plush ring holder, puffed satin lined, 7 extra good large pcs. in holders on bar, 10x 12¼x10.................Each, **$1.75**

IMPORTED WORK BOXES.
Fancy Celluloid Tops.

F6276    F6277

F6276—4¾x3¼, blue gray and sage green, imit. leather, padded hinged cover, Beidermeier design top and sides in colors, 3 piece fittings in holders, neatly lined. 1 doz. in box, asstd ....Doz. **75c**
F6277—6x4½, white enamel embossed scroll design, padded hinge cover with chromo picture under transparent celluloid, puff lined cover, diamond shape mirror, 5 fittings on hinged bridge, neatly lined. 3 in box, asstd. colors.................. ......Each, **18c**

IMPORTED CELLULOID
WORK BOXES.

F6276    F6277

F6276—4¾x3¼, blue gray and sage green, imit. leather, padded hinged cover, Beidermeier design top and sides in colors, 3 piece fittings in holders, neatly lined. 1 doz. in box., asstd ....Doz. **75c**
F6277—6x4½, white enamel embossed scroll design, padded hinge cover with chromo picture under transparent celluloid, puff lined cover, diamond shape mirror, 5 fittings on hinged bridge, neatly lined. ¼ doz. in box, asstd. colors.............. Each, **18c**
F6278—7½x5⅝, asF6277, 6 piece fittings, including scissors. ¼ doz. in box.
Each, **33c**

F6278

F6279—Wood frame box, red, green and tan embossed Mexican carved leather effect, asstd. colored pictures under transparent celluloid gilt metal corners, lock and key, puff lining, diamond shape mirror, 5 piece fittings, including scissors, 2 pin cushions, 6¼x4¾x3. 1 in box
Each, **35c**

F6279

No. 18K25223 Exceptional Value Fancy Sewing Box. Gilt finish with full celluloid top over very pretty pictures; brass corners; lined with very good quality material and diamond shape mirror on inside of cover; fitted with lock and key and contains six useful sewing articles. A very large and showy box, with plenty of room for such articles as thread, needles, silks and other sewing materials. Size, 9½x7x3½ inches. Shipping weight, 2 pounds.
Price, per set.....................**88c**

Fancy Shape Sewing Box.

No. 18K25231 Plush and Celluloid Combination Work Box. Top of box is decorated with very pretty picture under transparent celluloid; full mottled plush sides, floral design front and extension base; lined with sateen, inside of cover has a large mirror; contains six useful sewing articles, with plenty of room for other articles used by one who sews; brass catch and hinges. Size, 10x6½x4 inches. Shipping weight, 2½ pounds. Price, per set. **$1.42**

CELLULOID GLOVE HANDKERCHIEF OR JEWEL BOXES.

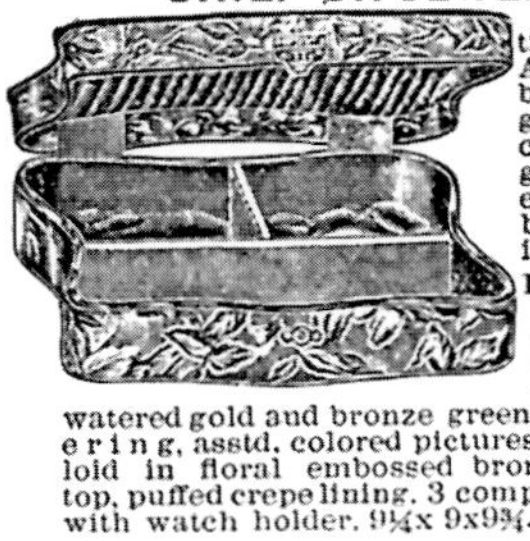

New and artistic shapes. All with embossed fancy gilt metal clasp and hinges. Sizes given are with boxes open. 1 in box.

F6466—Large red and white rose and leaf decorated watered gold and bronze green ground covering, asstd. colored pictures under celluloid in floral embossed bronze frame on top, puffed crepe lining, 3 compartments one with watch holder. 9¼x 9x9¾.....Each. **73c**

CELLULOID GLOVE, HANDKERCHIEF OR JEWEL BOXES.

New and artistic shapes. All with embossed fancy gilt metal clasp and hinges. Sizes given are with boxes open. Each in box.

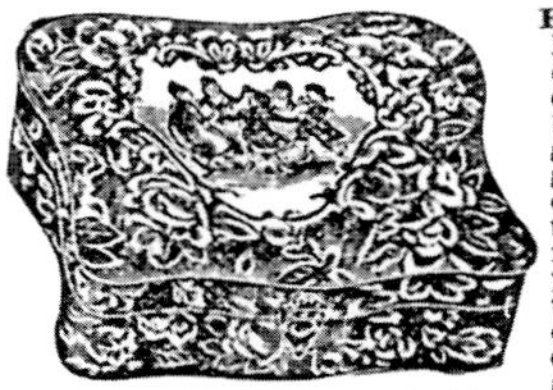

F6466—Natural color floral decorated bronze-green ground covering, tinted medallion pictures on top under celluloid, embossed gold frame, puffed mercerized crepe cloth lining, 9¼x9x10. Each, **73c**

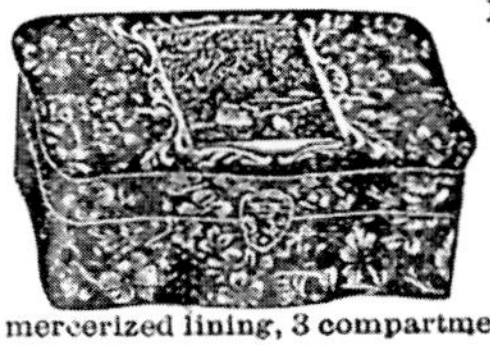

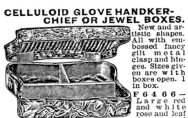

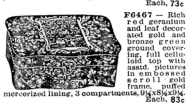

F6467 — Rich red geranium and leaf decorated gold and bronze green ground covering, full celluloid top with asstd. pictures in embossed scroll gold frame, puffed mercerized lining, 3 compartments, 9¼x8¼x9¼. Each, **83c**

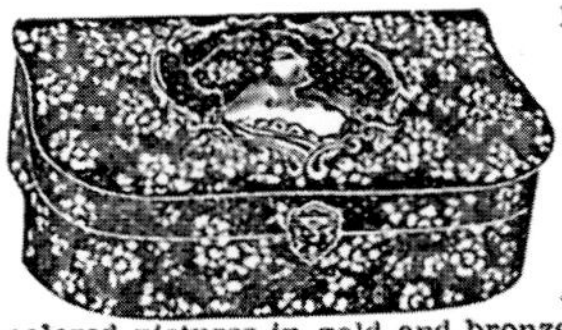

F6468—Dainty shaded violet decorated bronze green ground covering, full celluloid top with asstd. colored pictures in gold and bronze embossed dragon frame, fine puffed mercerized lining, 3 compartments, 11x8¼x8¾.............Each, **98c**

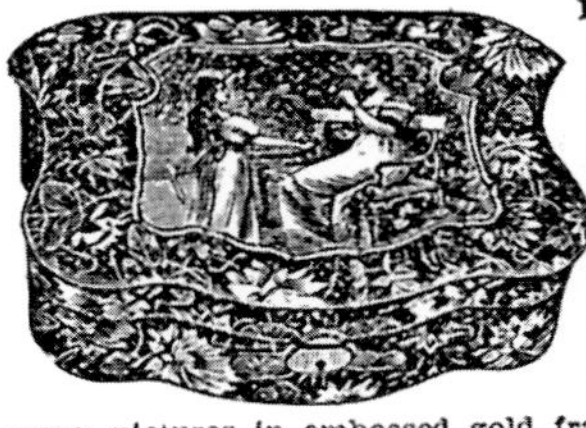

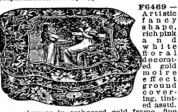

F6469—Artistic fancy shape, rich pink and white floral decorated gold moire effect ground covering, tinted asstd. group pictures in embossed gold frame, fine puffed satin lining, 4 compartments, 11¼x9¼x 10¼.................................Each, **$1.25**

CELLULOID BOXES AND NOVELTIES.

Asstd. natural color hand painted decorations. All silk bow tied.

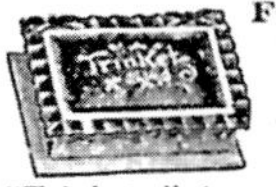

F6226 Asst—Square, oblong and diamond shapes, asstd. pink, blue and red, wreath design covering, crimped gold embossed edge, satin finish and transparent celluloid hand painted tops, "Jewels," "Trinkets," etc. embossed on cover, average 4x4. 1 doz. in box, asstd.......................Doz. **88c**

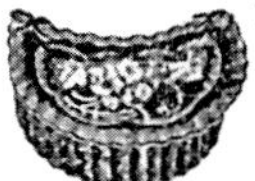

F6227 Asst—6 fancy shapes, pink, blue and red, satin finish and transparent celluloid sides and top with embossed crimped gold edge, hand painted floral decorated cover lettering "Jewels," "Trinkets," etc. on top, ribbon bow hinges, puffed embossed lining. 1/12 doz. in box, 6 in carton, asstd. Doz. **$2.10**

Satin Finish Celluloid GLOVE AND HDKF. SETS.

All with natural color hand painted floral sprays and gold tracings. Each set in box.

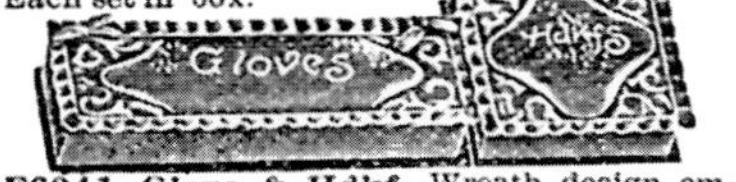

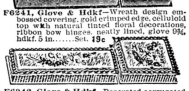

F6241, Glove & Hdkf—Wreath design embossed covering, gold crimped edge, celluloid top with natural tinted floral decorations, ribbon bow hinges, neatly lined, glove 9¾, hdkf. 5 in.......Set, **19c**

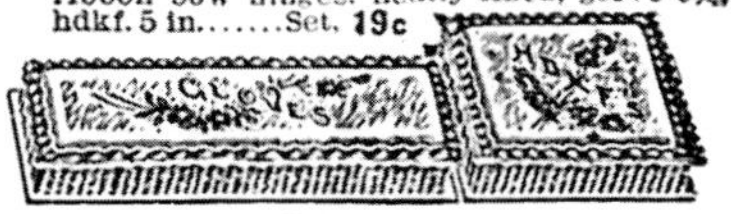

F6242, Glove & Hdkf—Decorated corrugated sides scalloped edge, hand painted gold traced floral decorations and lettering on top, asstd. pink and blue marble effect celluloid top, glove 10½, hdkf. 5½ in.. ..Set, **36c**

F6243, Glove & Hdkf—Asstd. pink and blue, gold celluloid, corrugated sides, embossed full crimped edge, hand painted floral decorated gold traced top, puffed embossed lining, 4 embossed brass metal feet, glove 11¾, hdkf. 6¼.... ....Set, **72c**

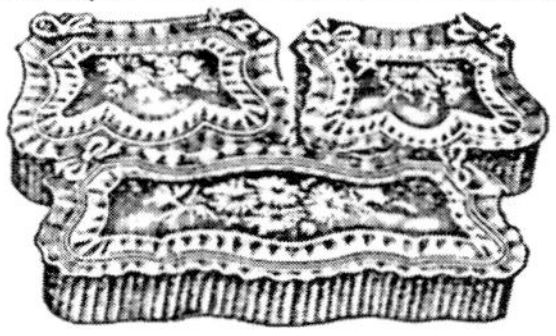

F6244 Glove, Hdkf & Trinket—Asstd. pink and blue satin finish, full celluloid, corrugated sides, embossed crimped gold edge and hand painted natural color gold traced floral decorations, ribbon bow hinges, glove 11¾, hdkf. 6½, trinket 5¼........ .Set, **★95**

TRANSPARENT CELLULOID NECKTIE CASES.

Ribbon bow tyings, all with fancy lettering, hand painted floral decoration. 1 in box.

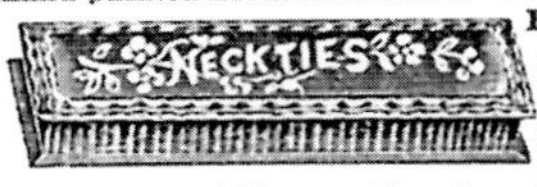

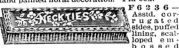

F6236—Asstd. corrugated sides, puffed lining, scalloped embossed asstd. pink and blue marble effect celluloid top. "Neckties," "Gloves," etc., 10½x4....Each, **18c**

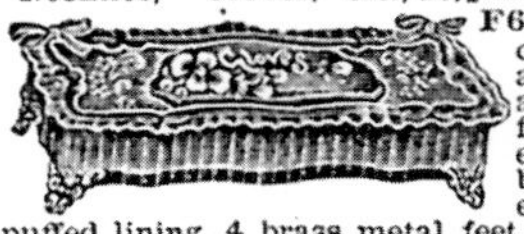

F6237—Full celluloid, asstd. pink and blue satin finish, crimped sides, embossed crimped gold edge, puffed lining, 4 brass metal feet, ribbon bow hinged, 9½x4½..........................Each, **36c**

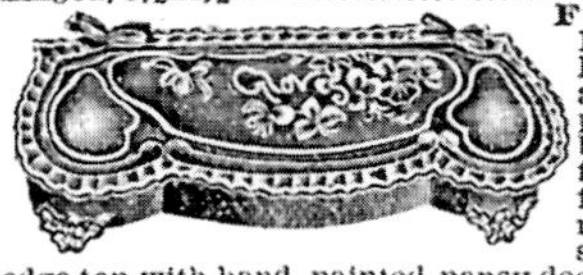

F6238—Full celluloid, asstd. pink and blue satin finish, fancy corrugated sides, gold edge top with hand painted pansy decorations, ribbon bow hinged, puffed lining, 4 metal brass feet, 11¾x4¾..................................Each, **39c**

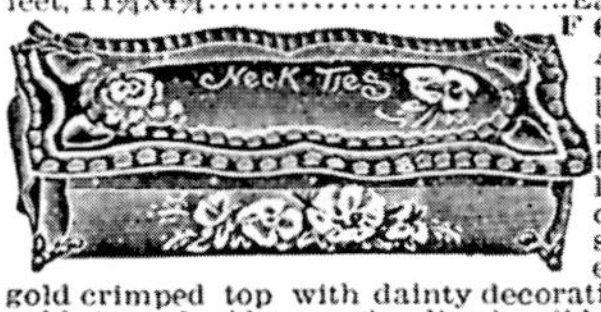

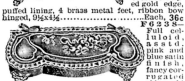

F6239—Asstd. pink and blue, satin finish full celluloid, curved sides and ends, gold crimped top with dainty decorations and gold traced sides, satin lined, ribbon bow hinged, 4 burnished brass feet, 12¼x5¼. Each, **73c**

CELLULOID GLOVE AND HANDKERCHIEF SETS.

Best values and most graceful and artistic shapes we ever offered. Each with hinged cover and embossed gilt clasp. 1 set in box.

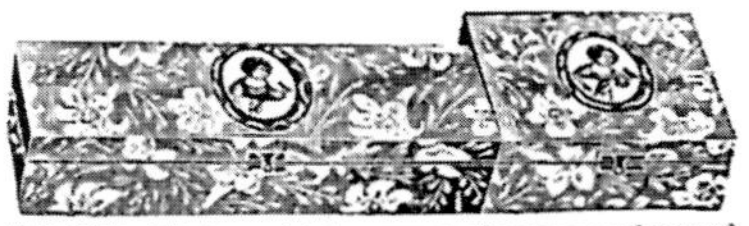

F6473—Flake gold, brown and green embossed Mexican carved leather effect covering, chromo picture in gilt frame, gilt ornaments, hdkf. 6x5¼, glove 10¾x3¼....Set, **18c**

A RARE VALUE AT 50 CENTS.

Will stand a BIGGER profit than most.

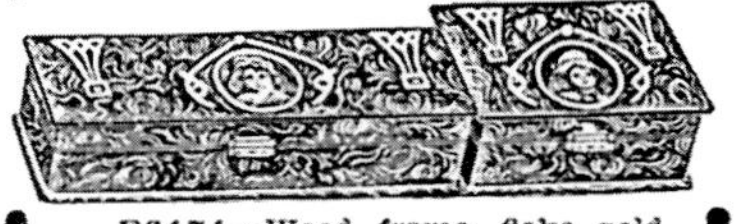

F6474—Wood frame, flake gold, brown and green Mexican carved leather effect covering, hinged extension cover, chromo pictures in gilt frame, gilt ornaments, gilt clasp, decorated to match. 1 set in box. Set, **37c**

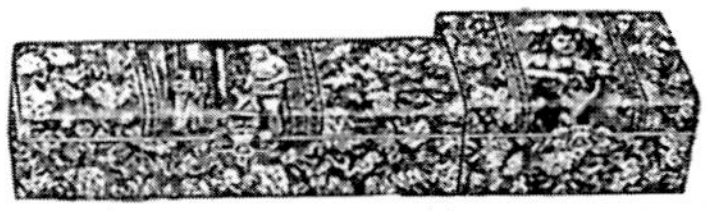

F6475—Asstd. colored gold trimmed floral decorated covering, asstd. colored pictures under embossed edge celluloid band on top, mercerized puffed lining, glove 12 in., hdkf. 6 in......................... ....Set, **68c**

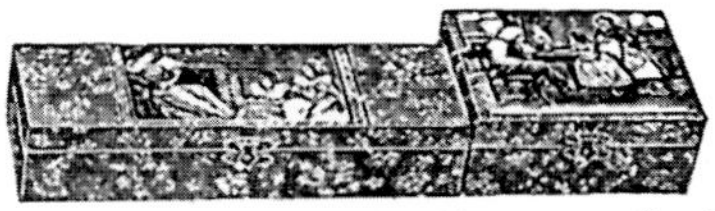

F6476—Dainty colored gold trimmed floral decorated light blue and green ground covering, rounded edge, full celluloid top over asstd. colored medallion pictures, good puffed mercerized lining, glove 12 in., hdkf. 6½ in..................................Set, **72c**

CELLULOID NOVELTY BOXES.

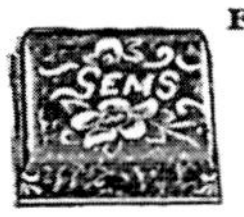

F6225, Trinket or Jewel—Asstd. pink, blue, yellow and green, opaque and mottled celluloid top, gold lettering and hand painted floral decorated, extension base, silk tied corners, 3¼x3¼. 1 doz. asstd. in box... .... Doz. **43c**

2 SPECIAL CELLULOID BOXES.

Rare values to offer as 10 cent leaders.

F6436, Glove or Necktie—American hand painted natural color floral decorated, asstd. pink, blue, yellow and green, opaque and mottled celluloid top, 8 silk tyings, extension base, 9¼x4¼. 1 doz. in box, asstd. Per dozen, **95c**

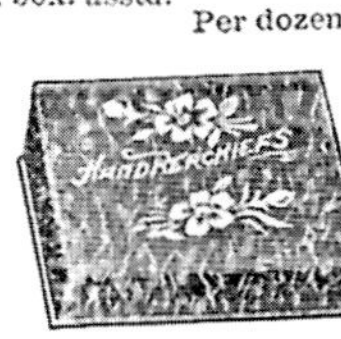

F6452, Hdkf. or Jewel—6¼x6¼, gold lettered tops "Handkerchiefs," otherwise as F6436. Per dozen, **95c**

Pricing Information

In this book, you will find an estimated *retail* price listed for each item. Price quotes are for similar items in very good to excellent condition. Adjustments in price should be made for wear, cracking, missing fixtures, etc. When determining the value of an item one must take into account the condition of the piece, its rarity, aesthetic appeal, and popularity.

At their best, prices are always controversial. However, collectors and dealers should realize that they are a guide. They are merely a starting point in determining a price and not intended to set them. Prices vary from one section of the country to another. Auction prices as well as dealer prices vary greatly and are affected by condition as well as demand.

Buy pieces you like and also buy quality. This is a winning combination and no matter what the fickle market does, you will still have a collection with which you will be happy.

Matching Pieces of Celluloid

It's always exciting to find celluloid items in the same pattern — a photo album that matches a toilet case or a handkerchief box and a glove box in a similar design.

Many collectors also try to match up their celluloid items with old framed prints, circular medallions, and other types of articles.

We have devoted the first group of photos in this book to matching items because we know collectors will enjoy seeing them grouped together.

Below is a wonderful stand photo album with matching post cards.

Millet's *The Angelus* framed print, glove or tie box, small matching handkerchief box.

Millet's *The Gleaners* circular medallion (also referred to as flue stop or cover), autograph book, work (sewing) box.

Photo album and matching work box.

Gallery of Celluloid Treasures

The following plate numbers, 1 – 124, feature matching pieces of celluloid.

Plate 1
Oblong photo album, 11¾"x9¼", $450.00 – 525.00.

Plate 2
Collar & cuff box, 6¼"x6¼"x5", $300.00 – 350.00.

Plate 3
Longfellow photo album, 7"x16", $500.00 – 600.00.

Plate 4
Upright photo albums, 8½"x10½", $450.00 – 525.00 each.

Plate 5
Upright photo album, 8¼"x10½", $450.00 – 525.00.

Plate 6
Collar & cuff box, 6¼"x6¼"x5½", $300.00 – 350.00. (See Plate 7 for matching design.)

Plate 7
Upright photo album, 10¾"x8¾", $450.00 – 525.00. (See Plate 6 for matching design.)

Plate 8
Jewel case, 12"x9½"x4", $500.00 – 575.00.

Plate 9
Musical photo album, 9¼"x11½", $550.00 – 625.00.

Plate 10
Collar & cuff box, 6¼"x6¼"x6", $300.00 – 350.00.

Plate 11
Toilet & manicure case, 10½"x5½"x4", $425.00 – 475.00.

Plate 13
Work (sewing) box, 9¼"x7½"x3½", $275.00 – 325.00.

Plate 12
Upright photo album, 8½"x10½", $450.00 –
525.00.

Plate 14
Shaving set, 7"x6½"x3½", $300.00 – 365.00.

Plate 15
Oblong photo album, 9¼"x11", $450.00 – 525.00.

Plate 16
Oblong photo album, 13½"x10½", $450.00 – 525.00.

Plate 17
Shaving set, 7"x6½"x3½", $300.00 – 365.00.

Plate 18
Necktie or glove case, 11¼"x3½"x3¼", $250.00 – 300.00.

F6456—Dainty tinted gold trimmed floral decorated light green and blue ground, asstd.
colored pictures under embossed edge, 4½ in.
celluloid band on top, mercerized asstd. colored lining, 6⅝x6¼x7⅜............Each, 35c
F6457—Round cornered top light blue ground,
gold trimmed asstd. colored floral decorated
covering, asstd. colored picture top under
celluloid, twilled mercerized lining, 6½x
6¼x7¼...............................Each, 36c

Plate 19
Handkerchief box, 6½"x6¾"x2½", $175.00 – 225.00.

Plate 20
Necktie or glove case, 13" long, $250.00 – 300.00.

Plate 22
Work (sewing) box, 9"x7"x4", $300.00 – 375.00.

Plate 21
Upright photo album, 8½"x10¾",
$475.00 – 550.00.

Plate 23
*Toilet & manicure case, 9¼"x8¾"x3", $450.00
– 500.00.*

Plate 24
*Toilet & manicure case, 11"x7"x7¾", $425.00 –
475.00.*

Plate 25
*Postcard/photo holder, 5½"x8"x2½",
$175.00 – 225.00.*

Plate 26
Oblong photo album, 9"x11½", $275.00 – 350.00.

Plate 27
Upright photo album, extra large, double clasp, 12½"x16", $425.00 – 500.00.

Plate 28
Collar & cuff box, 7½"x6½", $200.00 – 250.00.

Plate 29
Work (sewing) box, 8½"x7¼"x3½", $150.00 – 200.00.

Plate 30
Upright photo album, 8½"x10½", $300.00 – 365.00. (See Plates 31 and 32 for matching design.)

Plate 31
Oblong photo album, 9"x11½", $325.00 – 400.00.
(See Plates 29 and 30 for matching design.)

Plate 32
Same as Plate 31 with old matching print.

Plate 33
Collar & cuff box, 6½"x6¾"x6", $225.00 –
275.00.

Plate 34
Small jewel case, 5"x3¾"x2", $85.00
– 115.00.

Plate 35
Collar & cuff box, 7"x3½",
$275.00 – 325.00.

Plate 36
Handkerchief box, 6"x5½"x2¾", $110.00 – 160.00.

Plate 37
Shaving set, 8"x4¾"x3", $175.00 – 225.00.

Plate 38
Interior view of Plate 37.

Plate 39
Collar & cuff box, 7"x3½",
$275.00 – 325.00.

59

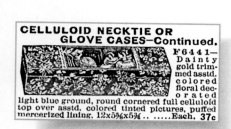

Plate 40
Necktie or glove case, 12¼" long, $185.00 – 235.00.

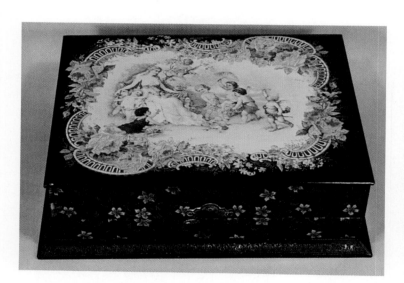

Plate 41
Toilet & manicure case, 13¼"x11"x4", $325.00 – 400.00.

Plate 42
Interior view of Plate 41.

Plate 43
Toilet & manicure case, 9¼"x6½"x4",
$225.00 – 275.00.

Plate 44
*Longfellow photo album, 8¾"x14",
$425.00 – 500.00.*

Plate 45
*Longfellow photo album, 8¾"x14",
$425.00 – 500.00.*

Plate 46
*Work (sewing) box, 7½"x5¾"x3", $175.00 –
225.00. (See Plate 49 for matching design.)*

Plate 47
*Necktie or glove case, 13"x4"x2½",
$185.00 – 235.00. (See Plate 48
for matching design.)*

F6427 — Full celluloid over rich asstd. natural color pansy decorated green bronze ground covering, 2 embossed bands round side and top, extension lid, lined with good puffed satin, 7x8x 10¾......Each, 92c

Plate 48
Collar & cuff box, 6"x6¾", $225.00 – 275.00. (See Plate 47 for matching design.)

Plate 49
Toilet case, 9½"x5"x2¾", $225.00 – 275.00. (See Plate 46 for matching design.)

F6602 — Dainty small pink and white rose decorated watered silver gold and bronze green ground, celluloid top over asstd. medallion pictures in gold frames, mercerized lining, 6 pcs. on hinged bar holder. 7⅜x7½x8. Each 69c

Plate 50
Work (sewing) box, 8"x6½"x3½", $175.00 – 225.00.

Plate 51
Work (sewing) box, 7½"x5¾"x3", $175.00 – 225.00.

Plate 52
Necktie or glove case, 13"x14"x32", $185.00 – 235.00.
(See Plate 55 for matching design.)

Plate 53
Upright toilet & manicure case, 11"x 5¾"x10½", $500.00 – 575.00.

F6569—Shaded red and white poppy decorated pebbled bronze green ground covering, figured silk plush covered sides and base, 9¼x4 celluloid covered compartment on top with medallion picture in embossed gold and green frame, double hinged doors in front with tinted medallion pictures in gold frames and embossed borders under celluloid, gilt pull celluloid front jewel drawer, extra good puffed satin lined throughout, silk cord trim comb, painted back mirror and brush, polisher, 2 salve boxes, bone handle file, cuticle knife, button hook, nkl. scissors, 19¼x10x 13½.. .... Each, $3.90

COMBINATION TOILET AND MANICURE CASES—Contd.

F6551—Moire effect lavender ground, violet and leaf decorated covering, celluloid top over asstd. tinted pictures in embossed Alice blue and gold frames, extra good mercerized lining, 9 pcs., painted back bevel edge mirror and bristle brush, comb, good bone handle file, cuticle knife and polisher, powder and salve box, nickel scissors, 11¼x 10x9½.. .. ..Each, $2.00

Plate 54
Necktie or glove case, 12½"x4", $185.00 – 235.00.

Plate 55
Upright photo album, 8½"x10½",
$300.00 – 350.00.
(See Plate 52 for matching design.)

Plate 56
Musical photo album, 9"x11½", $525.00 – 600.00.

Plate 57
Toilet case, 10"x5"x2¾", $375.00 – 425.00.

Plate 59
Jewel case, 11"x8"x2½", $225.00 – 275.00.

Plate 58
Upright photo album, 8½"x10½", $300.00 – 350.00.

Plate 60
Necktie or glove case, 12" wide, $150.00 – 200.00.

Plate 61
Handkerchief box, 5½"x5¾"x2½", $125.00 – 175.00.

Plate 62
Oblong photo album, 11½"x9¼", $425.00 – 500.00.

Plate 63
Oblong photo album shown with old print.

Plate 64
Oblong photo album, 11½"x9¼",
$425.00 – 500.00.

F6529 — Shaded cluster violet decorated bronze green and gold ground covering, celluloid top over natural tinted picture, extra good puffed mercerized lining, 3 pcs., colored decorated back bevel edge mirror and brush, white celluloid comb, 9¼x7¼x7.
Each, **$1.05**

Plate 65
Toilet case, 9"x5½"x3", $175.00 – 225.00.

Plate 66
Necktie or glove case, 11¼"x3½"x2¾", $185.00 – 235.00.

Plate 67
Toilet & manicure case, 11"x5¼"x2½", $200.00 – 250.00.

Plate 68
Upright photo album, 8½"x10½", $300.00 – 350.00. (See Plate 69 for matching design.)

Plate 70
Collar & cuff box, 6¼"x6½"x6", $200.00 – 250.00.

Plate 69
Stand photo album, 11¼"x18¼", $400.00 – 475.00. (See Plate 68 for matching design.)

Plate 71
Oblong photo album, 12"x9", $350.00 – 400.00.

Plate 72
Toilet case, 13½"x7"x2½", $225.00 – 275.00.

Plate 73
Interior view of Plate 72.

Plate 74
Stand photo album, 8½"x10½", $325.00 – 375.00.

Plate 75
Work (sewing) box, 13"x7"x4", $350.00 – 425.00.

Plate 76
Interior view of Plate 77.

Plate 77
Toilet & manicure case, 13"x8½"x3¼", $350.00 – 425.00.

Plate 78
Collar & cuff box, 6"x5", $150.00 – 225.00.

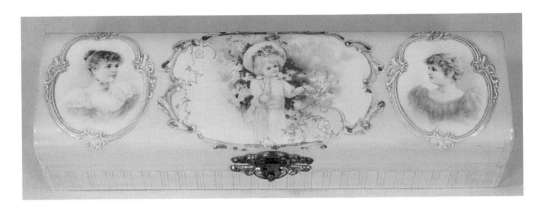

Plate 79
Necktie or glove case, 10¾"x3¼"x2½", $185.00 – 235.00.

Plate 80
Interior view of Plate 79.

Plate 81
Upright photo album, 8¼"x10¾",
$450.00 – 525.00.

Plate 82
Toilet & manicure case, 14½"x9¾"x3", signed Frances
Brundage, $425.00 – 475.00.

Plate 83
Work (sewing) box, 5½"x4½"x2¼", $175.00 – 225.00.

Plate 84
Collar & cuff box, 7½"x7½"x5½", $225.00 – 275.00.

Plate 85
Handkerchief box, 6"x5½"x2½", $110.00 – 160.00.

Plate 86
Handkerchief box, 5"x7"x2½", $125.00 – 175.00.

Plate 87
Collar & cuff box, 7"x5¾", $200.00 – 250.00.

Plate 88
Oblong photo album, 14"x10½", extra large, $375.00 – 425.00.

Plate 89
Necktie or glove case, 12¾"x4½"x2¾", $185.00 – 235.00.

Plate 90
Handkerchief box, 6½"x6¾"x2½", $150.00 – 200.00.

Plate 91
Manicure set, 9¼"x5½"x2½", $225.00 – 275.00.

Plate 92
Interior view of Plate 91.

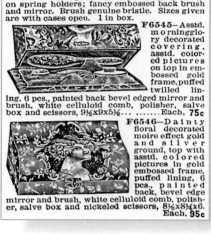

Plate 93
Toilet & manicure case, 13½"x11"x4", $450.00 – 525.00.

Plate 94
Toilet case, 13½"x5¼"x4", $400.00 – 475.00.

Plate 95
Autograph album, 6½"x4¼", $125.00 – 175.00.

Plate 96
Collar & cuff box, 7½"x7¼"x5¾", $275.00 – 350.00.

Plate 97
Hand mirror, 9¾"x4", $100.00 – 150.00.

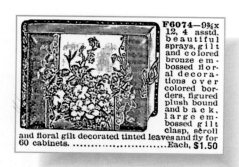

Plate 98
Handkerchief box, 7½"x5"x3", $150.00 – 200.00.

Plate 99
Oblong photo album, 11¾"x9", $350.00 – 400.00.

Plate 100
Necktie or glove case, 12¼"x3¾"x2½", $185.00 – 235.00.

F6568 — Heart shape, medallion picture and rose decorated top with gold scroll border under celluloid in beaded embossed gold frame, silk plush edges with 3 floral embossed gilt ornaments, rose wreath border around sides under celluloid with embossed edges, silk plush covered back, celluloid gold green and red trimmed bevel base, fine puffed satin lining, large painted gold trimmed decorated back hand mirror and brush, 2 salve boxes, polisher, comb, bone handle file, button hook, cuticle knife, nickeled scissors, 11¼x13x12.
Each, **$3.50**

Plate 101
Upright photo album, 8½"x10½", $425.00 – 475.00.
Shown with matching circular medallion (flue cover).

Plate 102
Toilet case, 10"x10"x2½", $225.00 – 300.00.

Plate 103
Upright photo album, 8¼"x10½", $425.00 – 500.00.

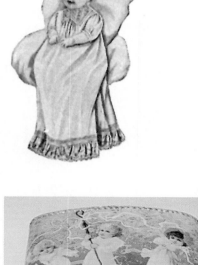

Plate 104
Work (sewing) box, 9"x5"x2½", $175.00 – 225.00.

Plate 105
Autograph album, 8"x5½", $100.00 – 150.00.

Plate 106
Collar & cuff box, 6½"x7½", $225.00 – 275.00.

F6562—Pebbled gold and bronze green ground, rich asstd. colored oriental covering, asstd. colored medallion picture tops under celluloid in embossed gold frame, jewel drawer with embossed gilt ring pull, puffed crepe lining, 7 pcs, hand mirror, brush, comb, scissors, polisher, salve box, file, 10¼x13½x 8½...................................Each, $1.42

Plate 107
Toilet case, 9"x6"x2½", $225.00 – 300.00.

F6570—Desk shape, full celluloid, automobile girls dressed in colored gowns, natural tinted features, in wreath of large violets with gold ground top, double embossed gold and color trimmed band edges, purple ends and front with fancy scroll and floral embossed gold trimmed ornaments, 2 drawers in bottom for jewels, trinkets, etc., one divided, heavy embossed gold plated drop pulls, good heavy puffed satin lining throughout, painted and gold trimmed back extra good bristle brush and hand mirror, comb, bone handle polisher, file and cuticle knife, 2 salve boxes, nickel scissors, 13¾x19¾x13¼. Each, **$5.75**

Plate 108
Toilet & manicure case, 17"x10¾"x9", $1,200.00 – 1,400.00.

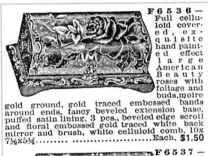

F6536—Full celluloid covered, exquisite hand painted effect large American Beauty roses with foliage and buds, moire gold ground, gold traced embossed bands around ends, fancy beveled extension base, puffed satin lining, 3 pcs., beveled edge scroll and floral embossed gold traced white back mirror and brush, white celluloid comb, 10x 7½x5¼........ ....Each, **$1.50**

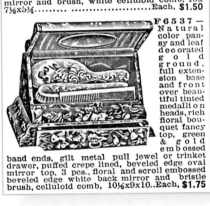

F6537—Natural color pansy and leaf decorated gold ground, full extension base and front over beautiful tinted medallion heads, rich floral bouquet fancy top, green & gold embossed band ends, gilt metal pull jewel or trinket drawer, puffed crepe lined, beveled edge oval mirror top, 3 pcs., floral and scroll embossed beveled edge white back mirror and bristle brush, celluloid comb, 10¼x9x10..Each, **$1.75**

Plate 109
Toilet case, 9¾"x5"x5", $150.00 – 200.00.

F6479—Celluloid top and front, natural asstd. shaded colored pansy and leaf decorated rich dark green background covering, top with asstd. dainty medallion pictures in embossed gold and oriental design frame, fine puffed satin lining, glove 12⅜, hdkf. 6¼ in. Set, **$1.50**

Plate 110
Jewel case, 9½"x7¼"x2¾", $175.00 – 225.00.

Plate 111
Necktie or glove case, 12¾"x4½", Millet's The Angelus, $175.00 – 225.00.

SAMPLE THIS NUMBER.
Special $2.00 advertiser.

F6478—Beautiful large tinted floral and leaf decorated bronze green covering, celluloid covered extension tops, asstd. colored pictures in gold & bronze, green embossed frames, extra quality mercerized puffed lining, glove 12¼ in., hdkf. 8 in.
Per set, **$1.25**

Plate 112
Handkerchief box, 6"x5¾", Millet's The Angelus, $150.00 – 200.00.

F6480—*Rare $3.00 value.* Celluloid extension half round base. waved top, shaded violet and leaf moire effect gold ground covering. top with asstd. tinted pictures in embossed gold and bronze green frame, best puffed satin lining, glove 13¾ in., hdkf. 8¾ in.
Set, **$1.85**

Plate 113
Work (sewing) box, 6½"x5", Millet's The Gleaners, $175.00 – 225.00.

Plate 114
Autograph album, 6" wide, Millet's The Gleaners, $100.00 – 150.00.

Plate 115
Same as Plates 116 & 117 with matching print.

Plate 116
Upright photo album, 8½"x10½", $450.00 – 550.00.

Plate 117
Toilet case, 13½"x7¼"x2½", $275.00 – 350.00.

Plate 118
Same as Plate 119 with matching circular medallion (flue cover).

Plate 119
Ox yoke photo album, 9¼"x11", $425.00 – 500.00. (See Plate 120 for matching design.)

Plate 120
Toilet & manicure case, 9¾"x7"x5½", jewel drawer in front, $275.00 – 325.00. (See Plate 119 for matching design.)

Plate 121
Work (sewing) box, 9¾"x8", imitation English Jasperware, $175.00 – 225.00.

Plate 122
Necktie or glove case, 12¾"x3½"x3", imitation English Jasperware, $150.00 – 200.00.

Plate 123
Collar & cuff box, 7"x5½", imitation English Jasperware, $225.00 – 275.00.

Plate 124
Jewel case, 8¼"x8¼"x3½", imitation English Jasperware, $225.00 – 275.00.

Plate 125
Musical photo album, 9"x11¾", $600.00 – 700.00.

Plate 126
Musical photo album, 9½"x12", $600.00 – 700.00.

Plate 127
Musical photo album, 9½"x13",
$650.00 – 750.00.

Plate 128
Musical photo album, 9½"x12", $500.00 – 600.00.

Plate 129
Musical photo album, 9½"x12", $450.00 – 550.00.

Plate 130
*Musical photo album, 9½"x12", signed J. L.
Loveday, $450.00 – 550.00.*

Plate 131
*Musical photo album, 9½"x12", musical
hardware made in Switzerland, $450.00 –
550.00.*

Plate 132
*Musical photo album, 10"x12½",
$650.00 – 750.00.*

Plate 133
Oblong musical photo album, 9¾"x12½",
$600.00 – 700.00.

Plate 134
Oblong musical photo album, 10½"x12",
$450.00 – 550.00.

Plate 135
Upright photo album, 12½"x16", extra large,
double clasp, $475.00 – 550.00.

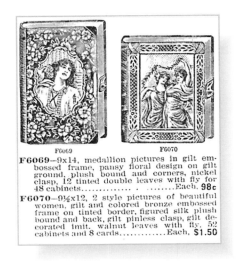

F6069—9x14, medallion pictures in gilt embossed frame, pansy floral design on gilt ground, plush bound and corners, nickel clasp, 12 tinted double leaves with fly for 48 cabinets............... . ...Each. **98c**
F6070—9¾x12, 2 style pictures of beautiful women, gilt and colored bronze embossed frame on tinted border, figured silk plush bound and back, gilt pinless clasp, gilt decorated init. walnut leaves with fly. 52 cabinets and 8 cards............Each, **$1.50**

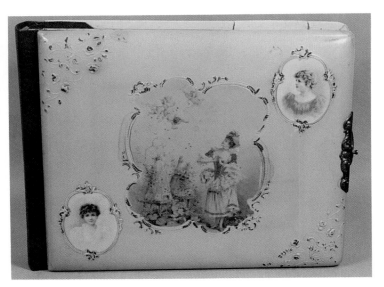

Plate 136
Oblong photo album, 10¼"x12¾", extra large, $475.00
– 550.00.

Plate 137
Upright photo album, 12½"x16", extra large, double clasp, $700.00 – 800.00.

Plate 138
Upright photo album, 12"x16", extra large, double clasp, $750.00 – 850.00.

Plate 139
Double photo album, 10¾"x16½", $700.00 – 800.00.

Plate 140
Oblong photo album, 10¼"x13½", extra large, $450.00 – 525.00.

Plate 141
Oblong photo album, 9½"x12½", $425.00 – 500.00.

Plate 142
Stand photo album, 10½"16", fold down with mirror in back, $575.00 – 725.00.

Plate 143
Stand photo album, 10½"17", $575.00 – 725.00.

Plate 144
Stand photo album, 12"x15½", $575.00 – 725.00.

Plate 145
Stand photo album, 11½"x18", $525.00 – 625.00.

Plate 146
Stand photo album, 10½"x16", fold down with mirror in back, $575.00 – 725.00.

Plate 147
Stand photo album, 10½"x16", fold down with mirror in back, $575.00 – 725.00.

Plate 148
Stand photo album, 16¾"x18", $800.00 – 950.00.
Two perfumes missing.

Plate 149
Stand photo album, 16"x17½", rare, holds two perfumes, $900.00 – 1,100.00.

Plate 150
Stand photo album, 8½"x11¾",
$350.00 – 425.00.

Plate 151
Stand photo album, 8½"x 11", $325.00 –
400.00.

Plate 152
Stand photo album, 11½"x17", $575.00 – 725.00.

Plate 153
Stand photo album, 11"x17", Mucha print, $525.00 – 600.00.

Plate 154
Oblong photo album, 8½"x12", $350.00 – 425.00.

Plate 155
Longfellow photo album, copyright 1901 McLoughlin Bros. N.Y., 7½"x16¼", $500.00 – 600.00.

Plate 156
Longfellow photo album, 7"x16", $450.00 – 525.00.

Plate 157
Upright photo album, 12¼"x16", extra large, double clasp, $600.00 – 700.00.

Plate 158
Ox yoke photo album, 9"x11½", signed Paul De Longpre, $325.00 – 400.00.

Plate 159
Longfellow photo album, 7"x16", $450.00 – 525.00.

Plate 160
Longfellow photo album, 7"x16",
$425.00 – 500.00.

Plate 161
Ox yoke photo album, 9"x11½", $325.00 – 400.00.

Plate 162
Ox yoke photo album, 11¼"x16½",
$525.00 – 600.00.

Plate 163
Longfellow photo album, 7"x16",
$375.00 – 450.00.

Plate 164
Ox yoke photo album, 12"x16½", $525.00 – 600.00.

Plate 165
Stand photo album, 14"x7½"x10½", unusual drop front, fan scroll design on sides, $450.00 – 525.00.

F6061 — 8⅜x10¼, 2 designs, landscape pictures in gilt and colored floral embossed frame, shaded border, tinted back, plush bound, gilt pinless clasp, 14 gilt decorated gray leaves with fly for 24 carbonettes and 16 cards.
Each, **78c**

Plate 166
Upright photo album, 8½"x10½", Mucha medallion print, $350.00 – 425.00.

Plate 167
Upright photo album, 8¼"x10½", $375.00 – 450.00.

Plate 168
Upright photo album, 8½"x10½", Mucha medallion print, $350.00 – 425.00.

Plate 169
Upright photo album, 8½"x10½", $225.00 – 275.00.

F6055—7¾x10 asstd. shaded fronts, colored medallion pictures in 2 style gilt embossed frame and floral designs, plush bound and corners, nickel pinless clasp, 12 tinted leaves with fly for 20 cabinets and 20 cards. 2 in pkg.......Each, 50c

F6055

Plate 170
Upright photo album, portrait medallion, 8½"x10½", $375.00 – 450.00.

Plate 171
Upright photo album, 8½"x10¾", portrait medallion, $350.00 – 425.00.

Plate 172
Upright photo album, 8½"x10¼", portrait medallion, $350.00 – 425.00.

Plate 173
Upright photo album, 8½"x10¾", portrait medallion, $350.00 – 425.00.

Plate 174
Upright photo album, 8¼"x10½", embossed raised design, $250.00 – 300.00.

Plate 175
Upright photo album, 8¾"x10½", $300.00 – 375.00.

Plate 176
Upright photo album, 8½"x10½", $150.00 – 200.00.

Plate 177
Upright photo album, 8½"x10½", $325.00 – 400.00.

Plate 178
Upright photo album, 8½"x10½", $325.00 – 375.00.

Plate 179
Upright photo album, 8½"x10½", $325.00 – 375.00.

Plate 180
Upright photo album, 8¼"x10¾", $350.00 – 425.00.

Plate 181
Upright photo album, 8¼"x10½", $350.00 – 425.00.

Plate 182
Upright photo album, 8¼"x10¾", $375.00 – 450.00.

Plate 183
Upright photo album, 8½"x10¾", $375.00 – 450.00.

Plate 184
Upright photo album, 8½"x10½", $375.00 – 450.00.

Plate 185
Upright photo album, 8½"x10½", celluloid floral design front & back, $375.00 – 450.00.

Plate 186
Upright photo album, 8½"x10½", $375.00 – 450.00.

Plate 187
Upright photo album, 8½"x10½", $375.00 – 450.00.

Plate 188
Upright photo album, 8½"x10½"
$375.00 – 450.00.

Plate 189
Upright photo album, 8½"x10½",
$375.00 – 450.00.

Plate 190
Upright photo album, 8½"x10½",
$325.00 – 375.00.

Plate 191
Upright photo album, 8¼"x10½", $325.00 – 375.00.

Plate 192
Upright photo album, raised floral design, 8¼"x10¾", $350.00 – 425.00.

Plate 193
Upright photo album, 8½"x10¾", $325.00 – 375.00.

Plate 194
Upright photo album, 8½"x10¾", $375.00 – 450.00.

Plate 195
Upright photo album, 8¼"x10½", $375.00 – 450.00.

Plate 196
Upright photo album, 8½"x10¾", $325.00 – 375.00.

Plate 197
Upright photo album, 8½"x10½", $375.00 – 450.00.

Plate 198
Upright photo album, 8¾"x10½", $525.00 – 625.00.

Plate 199
Upright photo album, 8½"x10½", $525.00 – 625.00.

Plate 200
Upright photo album, 8½"x10½",
$525.00 – 625.00.

Plate 201
Upright photo album, 8½"x10½",
$525.00 – 625.00.

Plate 202
Upright photo album, 7½"x9¾", $525.00
– 625.00.

Plate 203
Upright photo album, 8¼"x10½", $525.00
– 625.00.

Plate 204
Upright photo album, 8¼"x10¾", $525.00 – 625.00.

Plate 205
Upright photo album, 8½"x10½", $525.00 – 625.00.

Plate 206
Oblong photo album, 9½"x11", $500.00 – 600.00.

Plate 207
Upright photo album, 8¼"x10½", $375.00 – 450.00.

Plate 208
Upright photo album, 8¾"x10½", $375.00 – 450.00.

Plate 209
Upright photo album, 8½"x10¾", $350.00 – 425.00.

Plate 210
Upright photo album, 8¼"x10¾", $450.00 – 525.00.

Plate 211
Upright photo album, 8½"x10¾", $450.00 – 525.00.

Plate 212
Upright photo album, 8½"x10¾",
$450.00 – 525.00.

Plate 213
Oblong photo album, 9½"x11½", $300.00 – 375.00.

F6066 — Jack rose decoration with medallion picture in frame, under transparent celluloid front and back, gilt pinless clasp, 16 decorated tinted bevel leaves with fly, 28 cabinets and 16 cards....Each, $1.40

F6069 — 9 x 14, natural colored roses on gilt ground, medallion girl with pansies in embossed scroll and floral gilt frame, plush bound and corners, nickel clasp, 12 light green gilt decorated leaves, double openings, with fly for 48 cabinets....Each, 98c

Plate 214
Upright photo album, 8¾"x10¾", $325.00 – 400.00.

Plate 215
Upright photo album, 8"x10½",
$350.00 – 425.00.

Plate 216
Upright photo album, 8½"x10¾", $425.00 – 500.00.

Plate 217
Upright photo album, 8½"x10¼", Mucha print, $425.00 – 500.00.

Plate 218
Upright photo album, 8½"x10½", $375.00 – 450.00.

Plate 219
Upright photo album, 8½"x10½", $375.00 – 450.00.

Plate 220
Oblong photo album, 9¼"x11¾", Mucha print,
$375.00 – 450.00.

Plate 221
Upright photo album, 8½"x10¾", sou-
venir of Columbia Expedition 1893,
$350.00 – 425.00.

F6070—9½x12, 2 style
pictures of beautiful
women, rich gilt and
colored bronze em-
bossed floral and
scroll frame on tinted
border, figured silk
plush bound and
back, heavy embos-
sed gilt pinless clasp,
tinted beveled gilt
decorated leaves and
fly for 52 cabinets
and 8 cards.
Each, $1.50

Plate 222
Upright photo album, 8½"x10½",
$325.00 – 375.00.

Plate 223
Oblong photo album, 9½"x11½", $375.00 – 450.00.

Plate 225
Upright photo album, 8½"x10½", $325.00 – 375.00.

Plate 224
Upright photo album, 8½"x10½", $350.00 – 425.00.

Plate 226
Oblong photo album, 9"x11½", $375.00 – 450.00.

Plate 227
Upright photo album, 8¾"x10½", $400.00 – 475.00.

Plate 228
*Upright photo album, 8½"x10½",
$325.00 – 375.00.*

Plate 229
*Upright photo album, 8½"x10¾",
golfers, celluloid front & back, $450.00
– 525.00.*

Plate 230
*Upright photo album, 8½"x10½", auto-
mobile ladies, $525.00 – 600.00.*

Plate 231
*Upright photo album, 8¼"x10½", $350.00 –
425.00.*

Plate 232
Upright photo album, 8½"x10¾", $375.00 – 450.00.

Plate 233
Upright photo album, 8½"x10½", $375.00 – 450.00.

Plate 234
Oblong photo album, 9"x12", $350.00 – 425.00.

Plate 235
Upright photo album, 9¼"x11½", $275.00 – 325.00.

Plate 236
Upright photo album, 8½"x10¾", $300.00 – 375.00.

Plate 237
Upright photo album, 8½"x10½", $450.00 – 525.00.

Plate 238
Upright photo album, 8½"x10½", $300.00 – 375.00.

Plate 239
Upright photo album, 8½"x10¾", $300.00 – 375.00.

Plate 240
Oblong photo album, 9"x11½", $400.00 – 475.00.

Plate 241
Upright photo album, 8½"x10¼", $400.00 – 475.00.

Plate 242
Upright photo album, 8½"x10½", $400.00 – 475.00.

Plate 243
Upright photo album, 8½"x10¾", $350.00 – 425.00.

Plate 244
Upright photo album, 8¼"x10½", $400.00 – 475.00.

Plate 245
Upright photo album, 8½"x10½", celluloid floral design front & back, $350.00 – 425.00.

Plate 246
Upright photo album, 8½"x10½", $350.00 – 425.00.

Plate 247
Oblong photo album, 9½"x11¼", $275.00 – 325.00.

Plate 248
Upright photo album, 8½"x10¼", $400.00 – 475.00.

Plate 249
Upright photo album, 8½"x10¾", design in relief,
$325.00 – 375.00.

Plate 250
Upright photo album, 9"x11½", $450.00 – 525.00.

Plate 251
Oblong photo album, 8½"x10¾", $325.00 – 375.00.

F6058—8½x10¾, asstd. cowboy girl pictures in gilt frame, embossed colored bronze and gilt floral decorations, tinted front and back, plush bound and corners, fancy pinless clasp, 16 tinted gilt floral decorated leaves and fly for 28 carbonettes and 16 cards.
Each, 67c

Plate 252
Upright photo album, 8½"x10¾", $425.00 – 500.00.

Plate 253
Oblong photo album, 9¼"x11¼", $350.00 – 425.00.

Plate 254
Upright photo album, 8¼"x10¼", $375.00 – 450.00.

Plate 255
Upright photo album, 8½"x10¾", $300.00 – 375.00.

Plate 256
Oblong photo album, 9½"x11½", $375.00 – 425.00.

Plate 257
Upright photo album, 8½"x10½", $225.00 – 275.00.

Plate 258
Upright photo album, 8½"x10½", Maud Humphrey print, $325.00 – 400.00.

Plate 259
Oblong photo album, 9"x11", $300.00 – 375.00.

Plate 260
Upright photo album, 8½"x10¾", $350.00 – 425.00.

Plate 261
Upright photo album, 8¾"x10¾", velvet & brass trim with celluloid medallion, $275.00 – 350.00.

Plate 262
Upright photo album, 8½"x10½", $450.00 – 525.00.

Plate 263
Upright photo album, 8½"x10½", $450.00 – 525.00.

Plate 264
Upright photo album, 8½"x10½", $375.00 – 450.00.

F6057—8 ¼ x 10 ¾, 3 styles, children pictures and medallion heads in gilt embossed frames, asstd. tinted fronts and backs, plush bound and corners, fancy clasp, 14 tinted light gray gilt floral decorated leaves with fly for 24 carbonettes, 16 cards.
Each, 62c

F6057

Plate 265
Upright photo album, 9"x14", $375.00 – 450.00.

Plate 267
Upright photo album, 8¾"x10½", $325.00 – 400.00.

Plate 266
Upright photo album, 8½"x10½", $225.00 – 300.00.

Plate 268
Upright photo album, 8½"x10½", $325.00 – 400.00.

Plate 269
Upright photo album, 8½"x10¾", $375.00 – 450.00.

Plate 270
Upright photo album, 8½"x10½", $200.00 – 275.00.

Plate 271
Oblong photo album, 9"x11½", $200.00 – 275.00.

Plate 272
Upright photo album, 8½"x10¾",
$250.00 – 325.00.

Plate 273
Interior view of Plate 272.

Plate 274
Upright photo album, 8½"x10¾",
$200.00 – 275.00.

Plate 275
Upright photo album, 8½"x10¼",
$225.00 – 300.00.

Plate 276
Oblong photo album, 8¾"x11¼", $300.00 – 375.00.

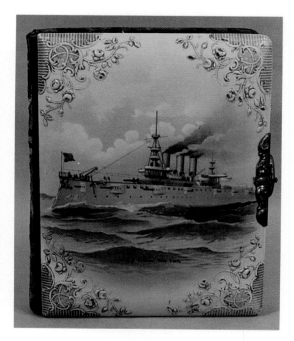

Plate 277
Upright photo album, 8¼"x10½", U.S. Cruiser New York, $250.00 – 325.00.

Plate 278
Upright photo album, 8¼"x10½", Battleship Maine, $250.00 – 325.00.
In Dec. 1897 the ship was sent to the Port of Havana to protect U. S. property. On February 15, 1898, the ship was sunk by an explosion. Two hundred sixty-six lives were lost.

Plate 279
Oblong photo album, 9"x11½", $225.00 – 275.00.

Plate 280
Upright photo album, 8½"x10½", $225.00 – 275.00.

Plate 281
Upright photo album, 8½"x10½", velvet with celluloid medallion, $200.00 – 250.00.

Plate 282
Upright photo album, 8½"x10¾", $200.00 – 275.00.

Plate 283
Upright photo album, 8¼"x10½", $200.00 – 275.00.

Plate 284
Upright photo album, 8½"x10¾", $200.00 – 275.00.

Plate 285
Upright photo album, 8½"x10½", $175.00 – 225.00.

Plate 286
Oblong photo album, 9"x11½", $325.00 – 400.00.

Plate 287
Upright photo album, 8½"x10½", $200.00 – 250.00.

Plate 288
Upright photo album, 8½"x10½", $175.00 – 225.00.

Plate 289
Small photo album, 4"x5", $75.00 – 110.00.

Plate 290
Small photo album, 6½"x8¼", $100.00 – 140.00.

Plate 291
Small photo album, 7"x8½", $100.00 – 140.00.

Plate 292
Small photo album, 6¾"x8½", $100.00 – 140.00.

Plate 293
Small photo album, 6¾"x8¾", $100.00 – 140.00.

CELLULOID PHOTO–Quarto.
All with gilt edge hinged leaves. 1 in box.

F6050   F6051

F6050—5x6, shaded front, embossed in gold, colored chromo center, leatherette bound, nickel clasp, 10 leaves for 22 cards. 6 in pkg.......... ....Each, **16c**
F6051—5¾x7½, 2 styles, shaded fronts with gilt and colored bronze embossed floral and bird design, asstd. landscapes, leatherette bound and back, plush corners, hinge clasp, 6 tinted leaves, for 10 cabinets and 6 cards. 6 in pkg... ....Each, **18c**

Plate 294
Small photo album, 5"x6", $100.00 – 140.00.

Plate 295
Small photo album, 6½"x8¼",
$100.00 – 140.00.

126

Plate 296
Small photo album, 6½"x8¾", $100.00 – 140.00.

Plate 297
Upright toilet & manicure case, 10¾"x4½"x10½", jewel drawer in front, $500.00 – 625.00.

Plate 298
Upright toilet & manicure case, 12½"x6"x13½", jewel drawer in front, $400.00 – 475.00.

Plate 299
Upright toilet & manicure case, 14"x9¾"x15½", jewel drawer in front, $1400.00 – 1800.00.

Plate 300
Upright toilet & manicure case, 14¾"x8½"x14",
jewel drawer in front, $1,400.00 – 1,800.00.

Plate 301
Upright toilet & manicure case, 15¼"x6½"x15½",
jewel drawer in front, $900.00 – 1,200.00.

F6566— Small pink shaded rose and leaf decorated gold ground covering, asstd. bust figures in front in embossed gold green and maroon trimmed frames, bouquet in basket under celluloid top with embossed edges, mercerized puffed lining, celluloid front jewel drawer, gilt metal pull, cord trimmed, 2 bevel mirrors on sides and door, 9 pcs., painted gilt trimmed back mirror and brush, comb, scissors, thimble, etc., 15¼x6x13......Each, $2.50

Plate 302
Upright toilet & manicure case, 11"x5"x14½", $325.00 – 400.00.

Plate 303
Exterior view of Plate 302.

Plate 304
Upright toilet & manicure case, 12"x7"x13", jewel drawer in front, $400.00 – 475.00.

Plate 305
Upright toilet & manicure case, 11"x7"x10¼", $475.00 – 550.00.

Plate 306
Upright toilet & manicure case, 12¼"x3½"x11¼", $400.00 – 450.00.

Plate 307
Upright toilet & manicure case, 11¼"x3¼"x12", $425.00 – 475.00.

Plate 308
Toilet & manicure case, 18½"x13¾"x10", $1,300.00 – 1,500.00.

Plate 309
Interior view of Plate 308.

Plate 310
Upright toilet & manicure case, 16"x5"x13½", unusual shape, $900.00 – 1,200.00.

Plate 311
Interior view of Plate 312.

Plate 312
Toilet & manicure case, 21½"x10"x10", very rare, all celluloid with velvet trim on jewel drawer, $2200.00 – 2,600.00.

Plate 313
Upright toilet & manicure case, 12¼"x6"x11½", jewel drawer in front, $400.00 – 475.00.

Plate 314
Toilet & manicure case, 16"x10"x7½", jewel drawer in front, $700.00 – 900.00.

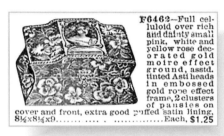

Plate 315
Toilet & manicure case, 8½"x6¼"x4¼", $350.00 – 425.00.

Plate 316
Toilet & manicure case, 17½"x5½"x8½", $450.00 – 525.00.

131

Plate 317
Toilet & manicure case, 16"x5¾", $500.00 – 575.00.

Plate 318
Interior view of Plate 317.

Plate 319
Toilet & manicure case, 17½"x10½"x6½", raised embossed rose design, $900.00 – 1,100.00.

Plate 320
Toilet & manicure case, 6½"x9½", $150.00 – 200.00.

Plate 321
Upright toilet & manicure case, 11"x7", $150.00 – 200.00.

Plate 322
Toilet & manicure case, 7"x10¼", jewel drawer in front, $200.00 – 250.00.

Plate 323
Toilet & manicure case, 10"x12", $175.00 – 225.00.

Plate 324
Toilet & manicure case, 13¾"x7¾"x7¾", jewel drawer in front, $475.00 – 525.00.

Plate 325
Upright toilet & manicure case, 8¾"x4½"x7¾", $375.00 – 425.00.

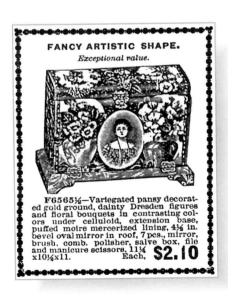

FANCY ARTISTIC SHAPE.
Exceptional value.

F6565½—Variegated pansy decorated gold ground, dainty Dresden figures and floral bouquets in contrasting colors under celluloid, extension base, puffed moire mercerized lining, 4½ in. bevel oval mirror in roof, 7 pcs., mirror, brush, comb, polisher, salve box, file and manicure scissors, 11¼ x10¼x11. Each, **$2.10**

F6567—Rich moire gold lattice ground, trailing chrysanthemums with foliage covering, fancy curved sides and extension base, asstd. Gainsborough ovals and floral baskets in green & gold traced frames under embossed edge celluloid, puffed satin lining, cord trimmed, 9 pcs., hand tinted white back mirror and brush, comb, polisher, salve box, file, scissors, button hook, tweezers, 19¾x 9x12¼..............Each, **$2.75**

Plate 326
Toilet & manicure case, 7"x13½", mirror in roof, $200.00 – 250.00.

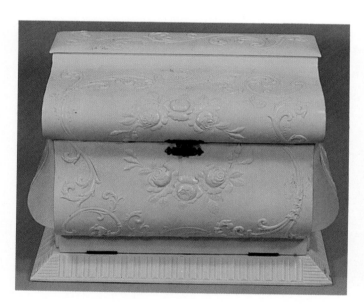

Plate 327
Upright toilet & manicure case, 12¾"x8"x9½", $325.00 – 400.00.

Plate 328
Interior view of Plate 327.

Plate 329
Toilet & manicure case, 9½"x12¼", $100.00 – 135.00.

Plate 330
Upright toilet & manicure case, 10½"x4½"x7¼",
$250.00 – 325.00.

Plate 331
Toilet & manicure case, 10"x10¾"x3", unusual shape,
$175.00 – 225.00.

Plate 332
Toilet & manicure case, 11¾"x6½"x5", $275.00 – 350.00.

Plate 333
Toilet & manicure case, 11½"x6½"x5½",
roll-top desk shape, jewel drawer in
front, $350.00 – 425.00.

Plate 334
Toilet & manicure case, 10"x6"x5½", jewel drawer in front, $275.00 – 325.00.

Plate 335
Toilet & manicure case, 13½"x7¼"x3½", $275.00 – 325.00.

Plate 336
Toilet & manicure case, 10¼"x 7¼"x2½", $175.00 – 225.00.

Plate 337
Toilet & manicure case,
13¾"x7¼"x3½", $300.00
– 375.00.

Plate 338
Toilet & manicure case,
13½"x7⅜"x4¾", roll-top desk
shape, $300.00 – 375.00.

Plate 339
Toilet & manicure case, 11"x11", unusual octagon shape, $110.00 – 150.00.

Plate 340
Toilet & manicure case, 13½"x8"x3¾", $300.00 – 375.00.

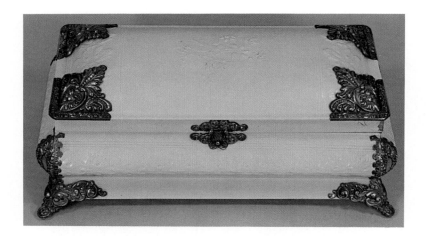

F6534 — Full celluloid, rich dainty shaded violet decorated bronze green ground covering, top with embossed bands and asstd. colored landscape in embossed gilt frames, bevel base, puffed mercerized lining, 3 pcs., painted back hand mirror and brush, white celluloid comb, 9⅜"x7¾"x4⅞"..Each, **$1.35**

Plate 341
Toilet & manicure case, 11½"x6"x4½", casket style with brass trim, $110.00 – 150.00.

Plate 342
Toilet & manicure case, 9¾"x5¼"x3¾", $110.00 – 150.00.

COMBINATION CELLULOID TOILET & MANICURE CASES—Contd.

F6552 — Large variegated pansies with foliage decorated gold ground, double embossed gold traced bronze green scroll banded celluloid top over colored Gainsborough heads, gilt metal pull celluloid front hdkf., jewel or trinket drawer, puff lining, 8 pcs., bevel edge white back mirror and brush, comb, polisher, file, curved point manicure scissors, salve and powder boxes, 10x9¼x9........ .. ..Each, **$2.25**

F6553 — Extra good large fittings, artistic shape, asstd. Savoy plush, richly tinted holly decorated ground under celluloid, colonial pictures in bright colors, beaded gold metal frame, fine quality puffed satin lining, 10 pcs., bevel edge floral embossed gold decorated white back mirror and brush, comb, file, knife, button hook, polisher, curved point manicure scissors, powder and salve boxes, 10¾x12½x11. Each, **$2.75**

Plate 343
Toilet & manicure case, 9"x7½"x3", $275.00 – 325.00.

Plate 344
Toilet & manicure case, 11¾"x8"x4½", raised cherubs & lady design, $250.00 – 300.00.

Plate 345
Toilet & manicure case, 13"x7¼"x3", brass trim mirror in roof,
$100.00 – 135.00.

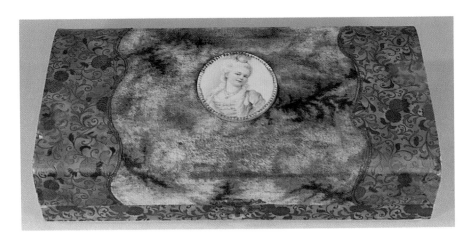

Plate 346
Toilet & manicure case, 13"x7¼"x3", brass trim mirror in roof,
$100.00 – 135.00.

Plate 347
Toilet & manicure
case, 9¾"x4¾"x3",
$100.00 – 135.00.

Plate 348
Toilet & manicure case, 13½"x7¼"x2¾", $275.00 – 325.00.

Plate 349
Toilet & manicure case, 12"x7½"x4½", roll-top desk shape, jewel drawer in front, $125.00 – 175.00.

Plate 350
Toilet & manicure case, 11"x5"x3¼", $200.00 – 250.00.

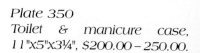

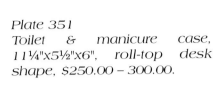

Plate 351
Toilet & manicure case,
11¼"x5½"x6", roll-top desk
shape, $250.00 – 300.00.

F6525 — Natural asstd. colored violet and leaf gold trimmed decorated covering, bevel base, slanting top with embossed fancy edge, celluloid band over dainty asstd. color angel pictures, puffed twilled lining, 3 pcs., bevel edge mirror, brush, white celluloid comb, 9⅜x7x4⅜ ....Each, 84c

Plate 352
Toilet & manicure case, 10"x6¾"x4", $225.00 – 275.00.

Plate 353
Toilet & manicure case,
11"x5¼"x7½", embossed design,
$125.00 – 175.00.

Plate 354
Toilet & manicure case, 9¾"x6½"x3½", $150.00 – 200.00.

Plate 355
Toilet & manicure case, 8½"x11", unusual shape, $300.00 – 350.00.

Plate 356
Upright toilet & manicure case, 8½"x5"x6¼", $325.00 – 425.00.

Plate 357
Upright toilet & manicure case, 10½"x6"x9", $275.00 – 325.00.

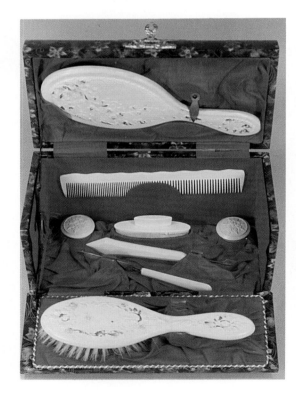

Plate 358
Interior view of Plate 356.

Plate 359
Toilet & manicure case, 14¾"x7"x3¼", has all original items,
$350.00 – 425.00.

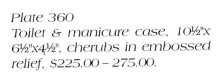

Plate 360
Toilet & manicure case, 10½"x
6½"x4½", cherubs in embossed
relief, $225.00 – 275.00.

Plate 361
Toilet & manicure case,
10"x7"x3½", $300.00 – 350.00.

Plate 362
Toilet & manicure case, 9¾"x5", $125.00 – 200.00.

Plate 363
Toilet & manicure case, 9"x5"x7", $275.00 –
325.00.

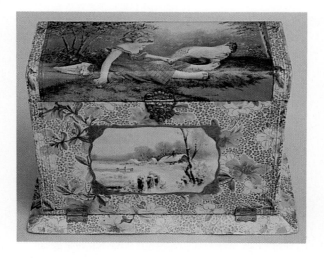

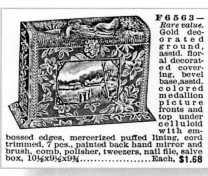

F6563—
Rare value.
Gold decorated ground, asstd. floral decorated covering, bevel base, asstd. colored medallion picture fronts and top under celluloid with embossed edges, mercerized puffed lining, cord trimmed, 7 pcs., painted back hand mirror and brush, comb, polisher, tweezers, nail file, salve box, 10½"x9½"x9¾....................Each, $1.68

Plate 364
Upright toilet & manicure case, 10½"x9½"x9¾",
$275.00 – 325.00.

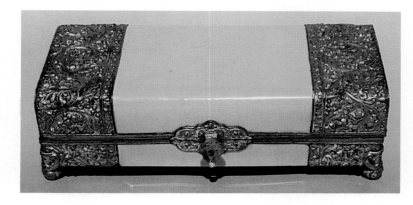

Plate 365
Toilet & manicure case, 10"x5"x3½", $110.00 – 130.00.

Plate 366
Upright toilet & manicure case, 8½"x5"x6¼", $325.00
– 375.00.

Plate 367
Toilet case, 10½"x6¼"x3", unusual shape,
$275.00 – 350.00.

Plate 368
Toilet case, 9½"x4¾"x2½", $175.00 – 225.00.

Plate 369
Toilet case, 10"x5"x3", $225.00 – 275.00.

Plate 370
Toilet case, 10"x7½"x3", $225.00 – 275.00.

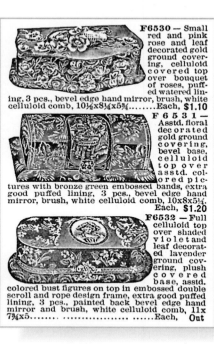

Plate 371
Toilet case, 10½"x7"x4¼", $200.00 – 250.00.

Plate 372
Toilet case, 10¾"x5¾"x3",
$200.00 – 250.00.

Plate 373
Toilet case, 10"x5"x3", $175.00 – 225.00.

Plate 374
Toilet case, 9¾"x4¾"x2¾", $225.00 – 275.00.

Plate 375
Toilet case, 10"x5¼"x2½", $150.00 – 200.00.

F6535—Full celluloid, rich natural asstd. colored carnation decorated goldground covering, top with asstd. tinted bust figures in embossed gold and green frames, puffed satin lining, 3 pcs., painted back hand mirror and brush, white celluloid comb, 10¾x8¾x5⅜. Each, **$1.50**

F6536—Bronze green and gold ground, natural colorasstd. pink and yellow rose and leaf decorated covering, full celluloid base and front over bouquet of roses with embossed gold trimmed edges, bevel edge oval mirror in roof, 3 pcs. painted back hand mirror and brush, white celluloid comb, gilt ring pull jewel drawer in bottom, puffed watered lining, 10½x5¼x10¼......................Each, **$1.75**

Plate 376
Toilet case, 5"x9½"x2¼", original matching items with decorated celluloid insets on mirror & brush, $250.00 – 325.00.

Plate 377
Toilet case, 11½"x6"x3¼", $250.00 – 300.00.

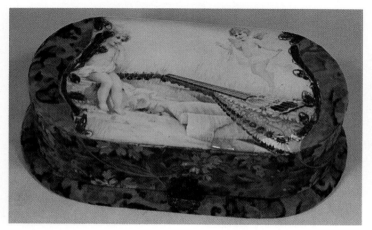

Plate 378
Toilet case, 10"x5"x3", $225.00 – 275.00.

Plate 379
Toilet case, 9¾"x5"x3½", $225.00 – 275.00.

Plate 381
Toilet case, 6¼"x9¾"x3¼", $275.00 – 350.00.

Plate 380
Toilet case, 9½"x5¾"x3¼", portrait Madame Recamier, $125.00 – 175.00.

Plate 383
Toilet case, 9"x6"x3½", $225.00 – 275.00.

Plate 382
Toilet case, 10¼"x5½"x3", $225.00 – 275.00.

Plate 384
Toilet case, 9"x4½"x3", $175.00 – 225.00.

Plate 385
Toilet case, 9¾"x5"x3¼", $175.00 – 225.00.

Plate 386
Toilet case, 9"x4¾"x3",
$175.00 – 225.00.

F6523 — *Rare*
$1.00 value.
Rich small
pink rose and
leaf gold trim-
med decorated
covering, quar-
ter round base,
embossed fan-
cy edge celluloid band round top over asstd.
natural tinted bust figures, twilled puffed lining, 3 pcs., bevel edge hand mirror, brush, white
celluloid comb, 9¾x6¾x4⅜..............Each, 75c

Plate 387
Toilet case, 11¼"x5½"x5", roll-top desk shape, $275.00 –
350.00.

Plate 388
Toilet case, 8½"x6¾"x3¾",
$225.00 – 275.00.

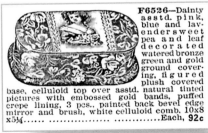

F6526 — Dainty
asstd. pink,
blue and lav-
ender sweet
pea and leaf
decorated
watered bronze
green and gold
ground cover-
ing, figured
plush covered
base, celluloid top over asstd. natural tinted
pictures with embossed gold bands, puffed
crepe lining, 3 pcs., painted back bevel edge
mirror and brush, white celluloid comb. 10x8
x5¼...... ....Each, 92c

Plate 389
Toilet case, 10"x4¾"x3", $225.00 – 275.00.

Plate 390
Toilet case, 9"x5¼"x2½", mirror in roof, celluloid medallion with paper sides, $75.00 – 100.00.

Plate 391
Toilet case, 10"x6¾"x4½", roll-top desk shape, $250.00 – 325.00.

Plate 392
Toilet case, 8½"x4"x3¼", $150.00 – 200.00.

Plate 393
Toilet case, 9¾"x5"x3½", $250.00 – 325.00.

Plate 394
Toilet case, 10½"x7½"x3", $250.00 – 325.00.

Plate 395
Toilet case, 9½"x4¾"x3¼", $250.00 – 325.00.

Plate 396
Toilet case, 11"x4¾"x3", $125.00 – 175.00.

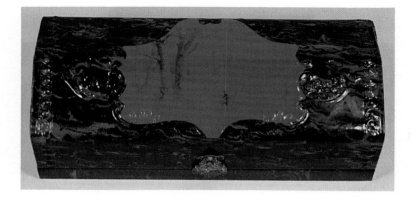

Plate 397
Toilet case, 9¾"x4½"x3½", $90.00 – 125.00.

Plate 398
Toilet case, 11"x7½", stamped on bottom patented Oct. 11,
1892, Dec. 27, 1892, Sept. 19, 1893, $75.00 – 100.00.

Plate 399
Toilet case, 10"x6¾"x5", roll-top desk shape,
$225.00 – 275.00.

Plate 400
Toilet case, 8¾"x7"x2½", $135.00 – 175.00.

Plate 401
Toilet case, 7"x6", $90.00 – 125.00.

Plate 402
Toilet case, 10"x7¼"x4¾", roll-top desk shape,
$135.00 – 175.00.

Plate 403
Toilet case, 11"x8¼", $250.00 – 300.00.

Plate 404
Interior view of Plate 403.

Plate 405
Handkerchief box, 5½"x5½", $40.00 – 60.00.

CELLULOID HANDKERCHIEF BOXES.

Very useful for jewel, hdkf. or trinket boxes. Each with hinged cover and embossed gilt metal clasp. Sizes given are with boxes open. 1 in box unless otherwise specified.

F6454—Imit. leather, asstd. colors, padded hinge cover, asstd. floral designs in natural colors, enamel effect, fancy gilt lettering, 6x6x2. 3 in box, asstd. Each, 15c

F6455—Wood frame, hinge cover, asstd. flake gold, brown and green embossed covering Mexican carved leather effect, chromo pictures in gilt frame with gilt ornament, neatly lined, 6½x5¾x6⅝. 3 in pkg. .... Each, 18c

Plate 406
Toilet case, 9¾"x5"x3¼", $90.00 – 125.00.

Plate 407
Handkerchief box, 5½"x5½", $100.00 – 135.00.

F6461—Full cellu-
loid over bronze
green ground,
rich red floral
decorated, bevel
base, top with
dainty asstd. col-
ored pictures in
floral gilt frame,
puffed satin lin-
ing, 7⅛x7¾x8¼.
Each, **$1.00**

Plate 410
Handkerchief box, 5"x7"x3¼", $100.00 – 135.00.

Plate 408
Toilet case, 8¼"x6", $75.00 – 100.00.

Plate 409
Toilet case, 8¾"x6", $135.00 – 175.00.

Plate 411
Handkerchief box, 7½"x6½"x2", novelty box with satin ribbon tyings & hand-painted cel-luloid top, $40.00 – 60.00.

Plate 412
Handkerchief box, 6"x6¼", $60.00 – 85.00.

Plate 413
Handkerchief box, 6½"x6½", $60.00 – 85.00.

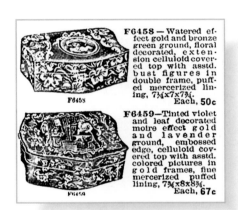

F6458 — Watered effect gold and bronze green ground, floral decorated, extension celluloid covered top with asstd. bust figures in double frame, puffed mercerized lining, 7¼x7x7¾.
Each, **50c**

F6459 — Tinted violet and leaf decorated moire effect gold and lavender ground, embossed edge, celluloid covered top with asstd. colored pictures in gold frames, fine mercerized puffed lining, 7¼x8x8¾.
Each, **67c**

Plate 414
Handkerchief box, 5"x7½"x3", $50.00 – 70.00.

Plate 415
Handkerchief box, 5½"x5½"x3", Mucha print, $175.00 – 225.00.

Plate 416
Handkerchief box, 5½"x5½"x3", $175.00 – 225.00.

Plate 417
Handkerchief box, 5½"x5½"x3", $175.00 – 225.00.

Plate 419
Handkerchief box, 6½"x6½", $100.00 – 150.00.

Plate 418
Handkerchief box, 5½"x5½"x3", portrait Madame Recamier, $175.00 – 225.00.

Plate 420
Handkerchief box, 6½"x5¾"x2¾", $90.00 – 120.00.

Plate 421
Handkerchief   box,   6"x8½"x3¾",
$90.00 – 120.00.

Plate 422
Handkerchief box, 7¾"x6¼"x2¾", $125.00 – 175.00.

Plate 423
Handkerchief box, 7½"x8"x3½", rare, dogs &
design in molded relief, $275.00 – 325.00.

Plate 424
Handkerchief box, 7"x5"x3½", rare, Indian print,
$275.00 – 325.00.

Plate 425
Handkerchief box, 6¼"x6"x2½", $135.00 – 175.00.

Plate 426
Handkerchief box, 5½"x4¼"x2½", $100.00 – 135.00.

Plate 427
Handkerchief box, 7¼"x7"x3½", $175.00 – 225.00.

Plate 428
Handkerchief box, 7½"x7½"x3", embossed cherubs in relief, $100.00 – 150.00.

Plate 429
Handkerchief box, 7½"x7½"3", $175.00 – 225.00.

Plate 430
Handkerchief box, 6¼"x6"x2½", $100.00 – 150.00.

Plate 431
Handkerchief box, 6½"x5½"x2¾", $175.00 – 225.00.

Plate 432
Handkerchief box, 8¾"x7"x2½", $75.00 – 100.00.

Plate 433
Handkerchief box, 6¼"x5½"x2½", $175.00 – 225.00.

Plate 434
Handkerchief box, 7¼"x6"x3", $150.00 – 200.00.

Plate 435
Handkerchief box, 6¾"x6½"x3", $150.00 – 200.00.

Plate 436
Handkerchief box, 5½"x5½"x3", $150.00 – 200.00.

Plate 437
Handkerchief box, 7"x6½"x3", $150.00 – 200.00.

Plate 438
Handkerchief box, 6¼"x6¼"x5", Little Boy Blue, $125.00 – 150.00.

Plate 440
Jewel case (trinket box), 5½"x4¼"x2¼", $75.00 – 100.00.

Plate 439
Jewel case, 7"x6½"x3", $175.00 – 225.00.

Plate 441
Jewel case (trinket box),
4¼"x4¼"x1¾", $50.00 – 75.00.

Plate 442
Jewel case, 8"x5"x3", $175.00 – 225.00.

Plate 443
Jewel cases, barrel shape, 3¾" wide, $60.00 – 90.00 ea.

Plate 444
Jewel case, trinket box, 2¼" wide, $40.00 – 60.00.

Plate 445
Jewel case, 9½"x7½", gilt lock, $90.00 – 135.00.

Plate 446
Jewel case, 9¾"x7½"x4", $125.00 – 175.00.

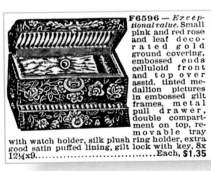

F6596 — *Exceptional value.* Small pink and red rose and leaf decorated gold ground covering, embossed ends celluloid front and top over asstd. tinted medallion pictures in embossed gilt frames, metal pull drawer, double compartment on top, removable tray with watch holder, silk plush ring holder, extra good satin puffed lining, gilt lock with key, 8x 12¼x9..................Each, $1.35

Plate 447
Jewel case, 8½"x5½"x3½", $125.00 – 175.00.

F6592—Asstd. pansy decorated clouded ground covering, embossed ends celluloid top over asstd. tinted bust figures in embossed gold and green bow knot design frame, puffed mercerized lining, watch holder, figured plush ring holder, 7x6x7½....Each, 50c

F6593—Asstd. pink and blue floral decorated gold moire ground covering, celluloid top over asstd. colored medallion pictures in gold embossed frames, puffed mercerized lining, 2 compartments, watch holder, plush covered ring holder, 7½x7¼x8........Each, 67c

Plate 448
Jewel case, 7¾"x5¾"x3", $125.00 – 175.00.

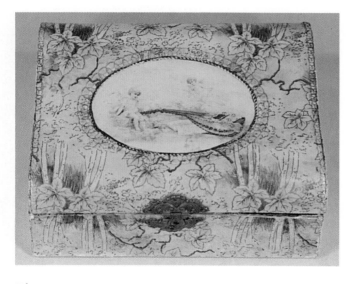

FANCY CELLULOID JEWEL CASES.
All with gilt embossed clasps and hinges.
Sizes given are with cases open. Each in box.

F6590
F6591

F6590—Colored natural floral decorated light moire ground, dainty pictures, puffed lining, watch holder, 6x5½x5¼......Each, 18c

F6591 — Variegated natural color floral decorated watered effect bronze green ground, colored pictures under celluloid in embossed gold frame, 2 embossed bands around top, puffed embossed lining, watch holder, 7x6¼x6¾..................Each, 35c

F6592 — Combination foliage and moss roses on light shaded ground "Floral Maiden" in embossed gold frame, raised band edges under celluloid, puffed mercerized lining, watch holder, figured plush ring holder, 7x6¼x7½..................Each, 50c

Plate 449
Jewel case, 9"x7¾"x3½", celluloid medallion with paper sides, $100.00 – 150.00.

Plate 450
Jewel case, 9"x3¾"x4½", $150.00 – 200.00.

Plate 451
Jewel case, 6¼"x5¼"x2¼", rare, Steeple chase scene, gilt lock, $175.00 – 225.00.

Plate 452
Jewel case, 8"x5½"x4", gilt lock & key, $100.00 – 150.00.

Plate 453
Jewel case, 8¼"x5"x3", gilt lock, $185.00 – 250.00.

Plate 454
Jewel case, 10½"x6"x4", musical, celluloid top with velvet trim, $200.00 – 275.00.

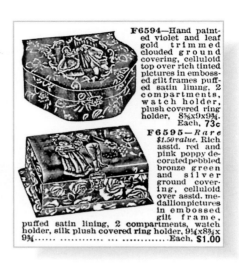

Plate 455
Jewel case, 6½"x4½"x2", $185.00 – 250.00.

Plate 457
Jewel case, 9½"x7¼"x2¾", $100.00 – 150.00.

Plate 456
Jewel case, trinket box, 4½"x1¾",
$50.00 – 75.00.

Plate 458
Jewel case, 9½"x8"x2½", all celluloid, mother-
of-pearl in border design, $175.00 – 225.00.

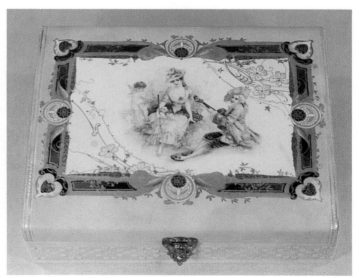

Plate 459
Jewel case, 8¼"x6"x3",
$125.00 – 175.00.

Plate 460
Jewel case, 7"x5"x3¼",
$185.00 – 250.00.

Plate 461
Jewel case, 10½"x6¾"x3¾", beveled mirror in roof,
$185.00 – 250.00.

Plate 462
Jewel case, 5½"x4¼", $185.00 – 250.00.

Plate 463
Jewel case (trinket box), 4½"x1¾", $50.00 – 75.00.

Plate 464
Jewel case, 10"x8¼"x4", double compartment
in top, removable tray, gilt lock, $125.00 –
175.00.

Plate 465
Jewel case, 7¾"x5"x3",
artist Jean Francois Millet,
$125.00 – 175.00.

Plate 466
Manicure set, 6½" wide, horseshoe shape,
$100.00 – 150.00.

Plate 467
Manicure set, 9"x5¾"x4¼", $275.00 – 325.00.

Plate 468
Manicure set, 6½"x6"x2¼", $175.00 – 225.00.

Plate 469
Manicure set, 10"x9"x3¼", $300.00 – 350.00.

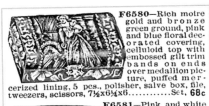

F6580—Rich moire gold and bronze green ground, pink and blue floral decorated covering, celluloid top with embossed gilt trim bands on ends over medallion picture, puffed mercerized lining, 5 pcs., polisher, salve box, file, tweezers, scissors, 7½x6¼x6............Set, 68c

F6581—Pink and white rose decorated watered ground covering, celluloid extension top over bright asstd. colored pictures in gold and floral embossed frame, puffed mercerized lining, 5 pcs., scissors, salve box, bone handle polisher, file, button hook. 7x8¼x7¼ ....Set, 72c

Plate 470
Manicure set, 9"x7"x4", $150.00 – 200.00.

171

Plate 471
Manicure set, 6¾"x4¾", $175.00 – 225.00.

Plate 472
Work (sewing) box, 7¾"x5¾", $40.00 – 60.00.

Plate 473
Manicure set, 7¼"x8"x3½", $175.00 – 225.00.

Plate 474
Work (sewing) box, 5½"x4¼"x2¼", $50.00 – 80.00.

Plate 475
Work (sewing) box, 3¾"x4¾", $125.00 – 175.00.

Plate 476
Work (sewing) box, 6¾"x5¾"x2¾", $150.00 – 200.00.

Plate 477
Work (sewing) box, 11½"x6¼"x4", $250.00 – 325.00.

Plate 478
Work (sewing) box, 5¾"x4½"x2¼",
$125.00 – 175.00.

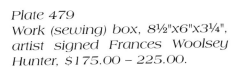

Plate 479
Work (sewing) box, 8½"x6"x3¼",
artist signed Frances Woolsey
Hunter, $175.00 – 225.00.

F6603 — Rich
shaded small
pink rose and
leaf decorated
bronze green
and gold
ground, cellu-
loid top over
tinted asstd.
pictures with
gilt bands,
diamond mir-
ror in roof, mercerized lining, 6 pcs. on hinged
bar holder, 8¾x7x7½.... ....Each, 73c

Plate 480
Work (sewing) box, 9½"x6½"x3½",
$90.00 – 125.00.

173

Plate 481
Work (sewing) box, 7¾"x5"x4", $135.00 – 175.00.

Plate 482
Work (sewing) box, 8"x6¼", $75.00 – 100.00.

Plate 483
Work (sewing) box, 8¾"x7", $150.00 – 225.00.

Plate 484
Work (sewing) box, 6½"x4½", $275.00 – 325.00.

Plate 485
Work (sewing) box, 11"x5¾", $250.00 – 325.00.

Plate 486
Work (sewing) box, 9½"x6"x4½", $125.00 – 200.00.

Plate 487
Work (sewing) box, 7"x5"x3", $100.00 – 150.00.

Plate 488
Work (sewing) box, 9¼"x7½"x4", $175.00 – 200.00.

Plate 489
Work (sewing) box, 8"x5"x3",
$150.00 – 200.00.

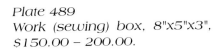

Plate 490
Work (sewing) box, 9½"x7"x3½", $150.00 –
200.00.

Plate 491
Work (sewing) box, 10"x7½"x5",
$250.00 – 325.00.

Plate 492
Collar & cuff box,
6 1/4" x 6 1/2" x 6",
$150.00 – 225.00.

Plate 493
Collar & cuff box, 6"x6¼"x5", $150.00
– 225.00.

Plate 494
Collar & cuff box,
6"x6"x4¾", Mucha
print, $150.00 –
225.00.

Plate 496
Collar & cuff box, 6⅝"x5", Mucha print,
$175.00 – 250.00.

Plate 495
Collar & cuff box, 6½"x5½", $100.00 – 150.00.

Plate 497
Collar & cuff box, 6¾"x6¾"x5",
$100.00 – 150.00.

Plate 498
Collar & cuff box, 7"x6", $200.00 – 250.00.

Plate 499
Collar & cuff box, 7¾"x7"x7½", handkerchief
compartment in bottom, $150.00 – 225.00.

Plate 500
Collar & cuff box, 7"x6½", handkerchief compartment in bottom, $200.00 – 250.00.

Plate 501
Collar & cuff box, 5"x6", $150.00 – 225.00.

Plate 502
Collar & cuff box, 6"x6"x5½", $175.00 – 250.00.

Plate 503
Collar & cuff box, 5¾"x5¾"x5", $150.00 – 225.00.

Plate 504
Collar & cuff box, 6¾"x7½"x6", $175.00 – 250.00.

Plate 505
Collar & cuff box, 6½"x7"x5½", $175.00 – 250.00.

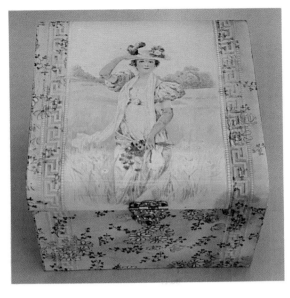

Plate 506
Collar & cuff box, 6½"x5", $100.00 –
150.00.

Plate 507
Collar & cuff box, 6"x6¾",
$150.00 – 225.00.

Plate 508
Collar & cuff box, 8"x7¼"x7½", handkerchief
compartment in bottom, $225.00 – 300.00.

Plate 509
Collar & cuff box, 7½"x7¾",
$175.00 – 250.00.

Plate 510
Collar & cuff box, 6½"x6¼", $175.00 –
250.00.

Plate 511
Collar & cuff box, 8¼"x7¼"x5¼", $175.00
– 250.00.

F6424 – Tinted
asstd. colored
gold trimmed
floral covering,
asstd. picture
tops under cellu-
loid, puffed mer-
cerized lined,
neat bow knot
design, asstd.
pink, blue and
green lining, 8x
8¼x10¼.
Each, 65c

F6424

Plate 512
Collar & cuff box, 6¾"x6½"x5",
$100.00 – 175.00.

Plate 513
Collar & cuff box, 6¾"x6½"x5", $100.00 –
175.00.

Plate 514
Collar & cuff box, 5"x7", $150.00 – 200.00.

Plate 515
Collar & cuff box, 8¾"x8"x5½", carved wood trim,
$200.00 – 275.00.

Plate 516
Collar & cuff box, 7½"x7"x5½", $100.00 –
175.00.

Plate 517
Collar & cuff box, 7½"x8"x5½", $100.00 – 175.00.

Plate 518
Collar & cuff box, 8"x7¼"x8", handkerchief compartment in bottom, $225.00 – 275.00.

Plate 519
Collar & cuff box, 7"x7½"x5½", $125.00 – 200.00.

Plate 520
Collar & cuff box, 7¼"x6½"x7¼", handkerchief compartment in bottom, $150.00 – 225.00.

Plate 521
Collar & cuff box, 6"x5", $150.00 – 225.00.

Plate 522
Collar & cuff box, 9½"x7"x6", button or jewel drawer in bottom, $175.00 – 250.00.

Plate 523
Interior view of Plate 522.

Plate 524
Collar & cuff box, 6¼"x6¼", handkerchief compartment in bottom, $150.00 – 225.00.

Plate 525
Collar & cuff box, 5½"x7½", $150.00 – 225.00.

Plate 526
Collar & cuff box, 6¾"x6", rare, $325.00 – 400.00.

Plate 527
Collar & cuff box, 5¾"x6¾", $175.00 – 250.00.

Plate 528
Collar & cuff box, 7½"x6"x7", $150.00 – 225.00.

Plate 529
Collar & cuff box, 9"x8"x6", carved wood trim, $200.00 – 275.00.

Plate 530
Collar & cuff box, 4¼"x4¼", fluted top with ribbon, hand-painted floral design, $75.00 – 100.00.

Plate 531
Collar & cuff box, 6¼"x5¼", $175.00 – 250.00.

Plate 532
Collar & cuff box, 7¼"x6½"x7¼", hand-kerchief compartment in bottom, $225.00 – 300.00.

Plate 533
Collar & cuff box, 7"x5¾", $150.00 – 225.00.

Plate 534
Collar & cuff box, 6¼"x6½"x6¼", $225.00 – 300.00.

Plate 535
Collar & cuff box, 6"x6"x5", $175.00 – 225.00.

Plate 536
Collar & cuff box,
7¼"x7½"x5¾", $100.00
– 150.00.

Plate 537
Collar & cuff box, 7½"x5½", $100.00
– 150.00.

Plate 538
Collar & cuff box, 7"x5¾",
$100.00 – 150.00.

Plate 540
Collar & cuff box, 7"x6½"x5",
$125.00 – 175.00.

Plate 539
Collar & cuff box, 10½"x6½"x5½", $250.00 – 350.00.

Plate 541
Collar & cuff box, 10¼"x6¾"x5½", $250.00 – 350.00.

Plate 542
Interior view of Plate 541.

Plate 544
Collar & cuff box, 6½"x5½", $90.00 – 135.00.

Plate 543
Collar & cuff box, 7¾"x7¼"x5½", $175.00 – 225.00.

Plate 545
Collar & cuff box, 8"x7"x5½", $100.00 – 150.00.

Plate 546
Collar & cuff box, 7½"x6", $100.00 – 150.00.

Plate 547
Collar & cuff box, 8"x7"x5", mother-of-pearl trim on border, $150.00 – 200.00.

Plate 548
Collar & cuff box, 10"x6½"x5½", $250.00 – 350.00.

Plate 549
Collar & cuff box, 6"x5¾", $175.00 – 250.00.

Plate 550
Collar & cuff box, 7¾"x7¼"x5½", artist
Paul De Longpre, $175.00 – 225.00.

Plate 551
Collar & cuff box, 10¼"x7½"x5½", $250.00 – 350.00.

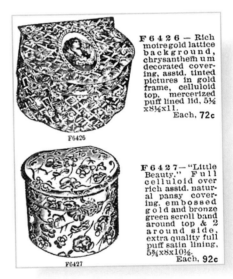

F6426 — Rich moire gold lattice background, chrysanthemum decorated covering, asstd. tinted pictures in gold frame, celluloid top, mercerized puff lined lid, 5½x8¼x11.
Each, 72c

F6427 — "Little Beauty." Full celluloid over rich asstd. natural pansy covering, embossed gold and bronze green scroll band around top & 2 around side, extra quality full puff satin lining, 5¾x8x10½.
Each, 92c

Plate 552
Collar & cuff box, 6¾"x6",
$150.00 – 225.00.

Plate 553
Collar & cuff box, 6½"x5",
$150.00 – 225.00.

Plate 554
Collar & cuff box,
8 ¹/₂ " x 6 " x 5 ",
$100.00 – 150.00.

Plate 555
Collar & cuff box, 6"x5¼",
$100.00 – 150.00.

Plate 556
Necktie or glove case, 14"x4¾"x3", $175.00 – 225.00.

Plate 557
Necktie or glove case, 12"x3½"x3", $150.00 – 200.00.

Plate 558
Necktie or glove case, 11¾"x3½"x3", $175.00 – 225.00.

Plate 559
Necktie or glove case, 12"x3½"x3", $175.00 – 225.00.

Plate 560
Necktie or glove case, 12½"x4"x2¼", $150.00 – 200.00.

Plate 561
Necktie or glove case, 11¾"x3¾"x2¾", $125.00 – 175.00.

Plate 562
Necktie or glove case, 13"x3¾"x2¾", $125.00 – 175.00.

Plate 563
Necktie or glove case, 12¼"x4¾"x3", $125.00 – 175.00.

Plate 564
Necktie or glove case, 13½"x4½"x3", $175.00 – 225.00.

Plate 565
Necktie or glove case, 12"x4"x3", $175.00 – 225.00.

Plate 566
Necktie or glove case, 12½"x3¾"x2½", $175.00 – 225.00.

F6441—Exquisite floral decorated gold ground, asstd, pictured in gold frames, embossed edge celluloid top, mercerized puffed lining, 12x4¾x5¾. Each, 36c

Plate 567
Necktie or glove case, 12½"x3¾"x2½", $200.00 – 250.00.

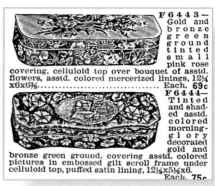

Plate 568
Necktie or glove case, 11¾"x4½"x2¾", $125.00 – 175.00.

Plate 569
Necktie or glove case, 13½"x4¾"x3", $125.00 – 175.00.

Plate 570
Necktie or glove case, 13½"x4¾"x3¼", $125.00 – 175.00.

Plate 571
Necktie or glove case,
13"x3¾"x2¾", $150.00 – 225.00.

Plate 572
Necktie or glove case, 12¼"x3½"x2¾", $200.00 – 275.00.

Plate 573
Necktie or glove case, 12"x4"x2½", $150.00 – 200.00.

Plate 574
Necktie or glove case, 11¾"x4½"x2¾", $200.00 – 275.00.

Plate 575
Necktie or glove case, 12½"x4"x3", $150.00 – 200.00.

Plate 576
Necktie or glove case,
12"x3½"x3", $150.00 – 200.00.

Plate 577
Necktie or glove case, 11¼"x3½"x2¾", $200.00 – 250.00.

Plate 578
Necktie or glove case, 14"x4½"x3", $200.00 – 250.00.

Plate 579
Necktie or glove case, 11¾"x4½"x2¾", $150.00 – 200.00.

Plate 580
Necktie or glove case, 10½"x6¾"x7½", jewel drawer in bottom, $125.00 – 200.00.

Plate 581
Necktie or glove case, 12¾"x4"x3", $125.00 – 175.00.

Plate 582
Necktie or glove case, 11¾"x3½"x2½", $125.00 – 175.00.

Plate 583
Necktie or glove case, 1 1 ³/₄" x 3 ¹/₂" x 2 ¹/₂", $125.00 – 175.00.

196

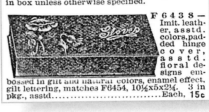

Plate 584
Necktie or glove case, 13¼"x3½"x3", $60.00 – 75.00.

Plate 585
Necktie or glove case, 13½"x3½"x3", $40.00 – 60.00.

Plate 586
Necktie or glove case, 12½"x3½"x3", $40.00 – 60.00.

Plate 587
Necktie case, 13½"x3½"x3", $70.00 – 90.00.

Plate 588
Necktie or glove case, 12"x3¾"x2¾", $90.00 – 125.00.

Plate 589
Necktie or glove case, 12¾"x4½"x3", $90.00 – 125.00.

Plate 590
Necktie or glove case, 13"x3½"x2½", $90.00 – 125.00.

Plate 591
Necktie or glove case, 11¼"x3½"x2½", brass corners, $90.00 – 125.00.

Plate 592
*Necktie or glove case, 12½"x4½"x4", jewel drawer in front, $90.00 –
125.00.*

Plate 593
Necktie case, 12½"x4"x2½", $100.00 – 150.00.

Plate 594
Necktie or glove case, 12½"x4"x2¾", $100.00 – 150.00.

Plate 595
*Necktie or glove case,
12½"x4¼"x3¼", signed Cather-
ine Klein, $100.00 – 150.00.*

Plate 596
Shaving set, 8¾"x7"x3½", $350.00 – 400.00.

F6390—Extra-
ordinary $5.00
value. Swell
sides, front
and top, tint-
ed wild rose
sprays with
foliage and
buds, gold
ground,
asstd. land-
scape tops
and fronts
under cellu-
loid, gilt
frames, bev-
eled exten-
sion base,
extra quality puffed satin lining, cord trimmed,
4¼x7½ mirror in back, 6 pcs., bone handle bristle brush, partition china mug, gold edge and
handle, floral decorated, 4 in. white back round
beveled edge ring handle mirror, corn knife,
white comb, warranted Sheffield razor, 9¾x20¾
x10¾...........................Each, $2.50

Plate 598
Shaving set,
5½"x6"x3¼",
$250.00 –
300.00.

Plate 597
Interior view of Plate 596.

Plate 599
Shaving set, 10¾"x7¼"x7½",
$275.00 – 350.00.

Plate 600
Shaving set, 9½"x6"x4½", $200.00 – 250.00.

Plate 601
Shaving set, 7"x6½"x3½", $175.00 – 225.00.

Plate 602
Shaving set, 9"x7¼"x4", $325.00 – 400.00.

Plate 603
Shaving set, 7¼"x6"x4", $175.00 – 225.00.

F6386 — Rich floral decorated bronze green ground, asstd. natural tinted picture tops under celluloid, 2 gold bands, extra quality puffed lining, badger hair brush, tinted and floral decorated embossed partition mug. 4 in. ring handle bevel mirror, 9x8½x7½......Each, **$1.23**

F6380½ — Asstd. picture tops in embossed gold frame, delicately tinted apple blossoms on bronze green moire ground, embossed puffed lining, bristle brush, partition floral decorated mug, gold edge and handle, 6½x9x6¼. Each, **48c**

Plate 604
Shaving set, 9¾"x6"x5", $250.00 – 325.00.

F6385 — Beveled extension base, large pink and white rosebud decorated silver, gold and bronze green moire effect ground covering, beaded edge, celluloid top with bouquet in embossed gold frame, puffed satin lining, 5x6¾ mirror in roof, white enamel handle bristle brush, gold showered handle and edge floral decorated partition mug, 8¾x10¼x6¼................ Each, **92c**

Plate 605
Shaving set, 9½"x7½"x4", $250.00 – 325.00.

Plate 606
Postcard case, 8½"x6½"x3½", $125.00 – 175.00.

Plate 607
Postcard album, 8"x4¾", $100.00 – 135.00.

Plate 608
Interior view of Plate 607.

F6502—Asstd. natural color clematis decorated dark mottled background covering, 3 landscape post cards on top under embossed border celluloid cover, gilt name "Post Cards" in embossed gold frame. 3 compartments, 12⅜x7¾x8¼......Each, 73c

Plate 609
Postcard album, 7½"x4¾", $100.00 – 135.00.

Plate 610
Letter box, 9¾"x6¼"x4¼", $275.00 – 325.00.

Plate 611
Letter box, 7½"x7½"x3½", $200.00 – 275.00.

Plate 612
Letter box, 9½"x7½"x3", $275.00 – 325.00.

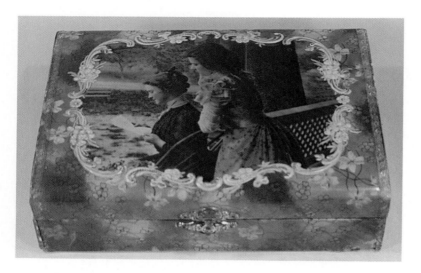

Plate 613
Letter box, 11"x8"x3", $275.00 – 325.00.

Plate 614
Letter box, 9½"x7¼"x2¾", $200.00 – 275.00.

Plate 615
Cabinet photo holder, 6¾"x4½"x8½", $250.00 – 325.00.

F6487 — Maroon background, fancy scroll decorated covering, embossed edges, celluloid top with green and bronze decorated embossed "Photo" and floral design, mercerized asstd. colored puffed lining. 8⅛x7¼ x3⅜.....................Each, 48c

Plate 616
Photo case, 8¼"x6½"x3", $90.00 – 125.00.

Plate 617
Letter box, 6"x7½"x2", $100.00 – 150.00.

Plate 618
Smokers' set, 8"x4"x2½", $90.00 – 125.00.

Plate 619
Interior view of Plate 618.

Plate 620
Smokers' set, 7½"x5"x2½", $100.00 – 175.00.

Plate 621
Smokers' set, 8¼"x5¾"x2½", $175.00 – 225.00.

Plate 622
Smokers' set, 6½"x4½"x2", $150.00 – 200.00.

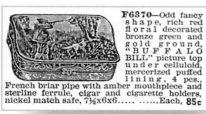

Plate 623
Smokers' set, 6¾"x6½"x2½", $150.00 – 200.00.

Plate 624
Autograph album, 4½"x3", in original box,
$100.00 – 150.00.

Plate 625
Autograph album, 4¾"x2¾", $75.00 – 125.00.

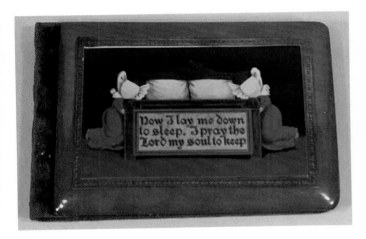

Plate 626
Autograph album, 6½"x4¼", $175.00 – 225.00.

Plate 627
Autograph album, 6½"x5", $175.00 – 225.00.

Plate 628
Autograph album, 6½"x4¼", $175.00 – 225.00.

Plate 629
Autograph album, 4½"x6", $125.00 – 175.00.

Plate 630
Autograph albums, $60.00 – 125.00 each.

Plate 631
Autograph album, 6¼"x4¼", $100.00 – 150.00.

CELLULOID AUTOGRAPH ALBUMS.
⅙ doz. in box, asstd.

F6104   F6105

F6104—3 styles transparent celluloid fronts, asstd. colored photos, floral sprays and angels, imit. leather back, 60 tinted pages, fly leaf front and back, 4¼x6⅝......Doz. $2.00
F6105—As F6104, 5x7¾..............Doz. $2.25

Plate 632
Autograph albums, $60.00 – 90.00 each.

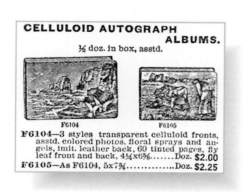

CELLULOID AUTOGRAPH ALBUMS.
⅙ doz. in box, asstd.

F6104   F6105

F6104—3 styles transparent celluloid fronts, asstd. colored photos, floral sprays and angels, imit. leather back, 60 tinted pages, fly leaf front and back, 4¼x6⅝......Doz. $2.00
F6105—As F6104, 5x7¾..............Doz. $2.25

Plate 633
Autograph album, 6½"x4¾", $175.00 – 225.00.

Plate 635
Autograph album, 4¼"x3", $60.00 – 90.00.

Plate 634
Autograph album, 6½"x4¼", $175.00 – 225.00.

Plate 636
Autograph album, 6½"x4¼", dated
1906, $175.00 – 225.00.

Plate 637
Autograph album, 6¼"x4¼", $75.00 – 125.00.

Plate 638
Autograph album, 6¼"x4½", $75.00 – 125.00.

Plate 639
Autograph album, 6"x4", $75.00 – 125.00.

Plate 640
Autograph album, 6"x3¾", $75.00 – 125.00.

Plate 641
Autograph album, 6¼"x4½", dated 1904, $175.00 – 225.00.

Plate 642
Autograph album, 6½"x4¼", $175.00 – 225.00.

Plate 643
*Autograph album, 7¾"x5",
$150.00 – 200.00.*

Plate 644
*Autograph album, 6½"x4¼",
$150.00 – 200.00.*

Plate 645
Autograph album, 6¼"x4½", $75.00 – 125.00.

Plate 646
*Autograph album, 6½"x4½",
$75.00 – 125.00.*

Plate 647
Autograph album, 6¼"x4½", dated 1910, $75.00 – 125.00.

Plate 648
Autograph album, 4¼"x3", $60.00 – 90.00.

Plate 649
Autograph album, 6¾"x4¼", $175.00 – 225.00.

Plate 650
*Autograph   album,   6½"x4¼",
$150.00 – 200.00.*

Plate 651
Autograph album, 7"x4½",
$150.00 – 200.00.

Plate 652
Autograph album, 6½"x4¼",
$150.00 – 200.00.

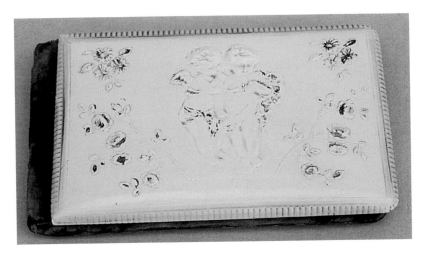

Plate 653
Autograph album, 6¼"x4", $40.00 – 60.00.

213

Plate 654
Autograph album, 6¼"x4¼", $40.00 – 60.00.

Plate 655
Autograph album, 4¼"x3", $60.00 – 90.00.

Plate 656
Autograph album, 4"x2¾", dated 1901, $30.00 – 50.00.

Plate 657
Autograph album, 5½"x5¼", $175.00 – 225.00.

Plate 658
Autograph album, 5½"x5", portrait Anna Potocka, $175.00 – 225.00.

Plate 659
Autograph album, 5¼"x5¼", $150.00 – 200.00.

Plate 660
Autograph album, 5½"x5", $125.00 – 175.00.

Plate 661
Triplicate toilet & shaving mirror, 10¾"x8½" each section, $475.00 – 600.00.

Plate 662
Close-up view of Plate 661.

Plate 663
Close-up view of Plate 661.

Plate 664
Triplicate toilet & shaving mirror, 20"x8¾" full size open, $600.00 – 750.00.

Plate 665
Triplicate toilet & shaving mirror, 10¼"x8¼" each section, $475.00 – 600.00.

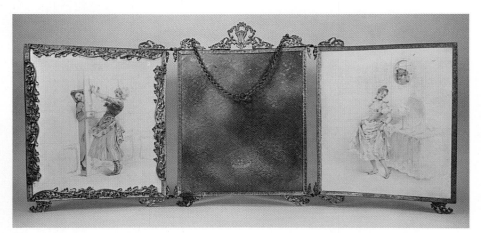

Plate 666
Triplicate toilet & shaving mirror, 20"x8¾" full size open, $600.00 – 750.00.

Plate 667
Triplicate toilet & shaving mirror, 23½"x9" full size open, $475.00 – 550.00.

Plate 668
Triplicate toilet & shaving mirror, 34"x11"
full size open, $450.00 – 550.00.

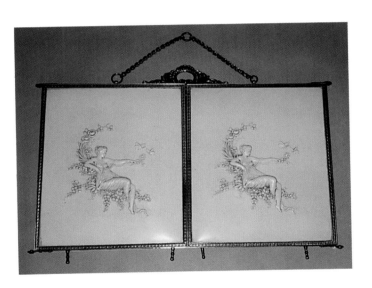

N1152—With lithographed picture back, 7x9, overlapping nickeled frame chain hanger. Asstd. backs. ⅓ doz. in box......Doz. **$1.35**
N1151—8x10, otherwise as N1152. ⅓ doz. in box...................... .. ..Doz. **$1.75**

Plate 669
Triplicate toilet & shaving mirror, 20½"x12¼" full
size open, $450.00 – 550.00.

Plate 670
Triplicate toilet & shaving mirror, 22½"x10¼" full size open, $475.00 –
550.00.

Plate 671
Triplicate toilet & shaving mirror, 20"x8¾" full size open,
$500.00 – 600.00.

Plate 673
Triplicate toilet & shaving mirror, $425.00 – 475.00.

Plate 672
Triplicate toilet & shaving mirror,
30¼"x10½", front feet allows mirror to
tilt, extends to 37". $450.00 – 550.00.

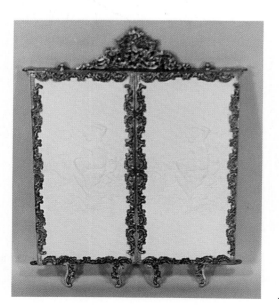

Plate 674
Triplicate toilet & shaving mirror,
$450.00 – 550.00.

Plate 675
Triplicate toilet & shaving mirror, 25½"x12½"
full size open, $500.00 – 600.00.

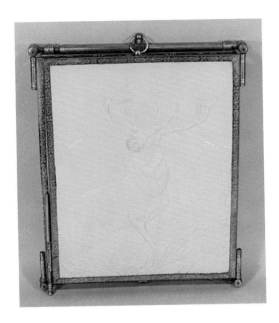

Plate 676
Triplicate toilet & shaving mirror, 32"x11"
full size open, $450.00 – 550.00.

Plate 677
Hand mirror, $40.00 – 60.00.

Plate 678
Brush, $100.00 – 150.00.

Plate 679
Hand mirror, $150.00 – 225.00.

Plate 680
Brush, 8½" long,
$90.00 – 125.00.

Plate 681
Mirror/brush set, $200.00 – 300.00.

Plate 682
Mirror/brush set, with manicure implements, button
hook, $250.00 – 300.00.

Plate 683
Hand mirror, $60.00 – 90.00.

Plate 684
Hand mirror, $125.00 – 200.00.

Plate 685
Brush, $100.00 – 150.00.

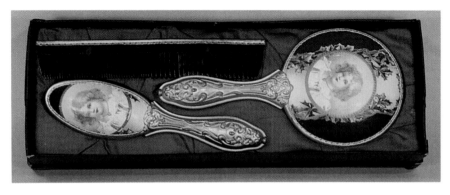

Plate 686
Mirror/brush/comb set, in original box, $350.00 – 450.00.

Plate 687
Hand mirror, $150.00 – 225.00.

Plate 688
Hand mirror, $50.00 – 100.00.

Plate 689
Hand mirror, $75.00 – 125.00.

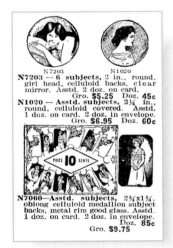

Plate 690
Pocket mirror, 2¼",
$35.00 – 75.00.

Plate 691
Pocket mirror assortment (advertising), $150.00 –
250.00 each. Upper left corner watch FOB, $250.00
– 300.00.

Plate 692
Pocket mirror assortment (advertising),
$150.00 – 250.00 each.

Plate 693
Mirror on stick, $85.00 – 150.00 each.
Bottom center large mirror, rare size, $175.00 – 250.00.

Plate 695
Tape measure, 1¾"x wide (advertising), portrait Queen Louise, $100.00 – 175.00.

Plate 696
Reverse view of Plate 695.

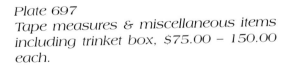

Plate 694
Pocket mirror assortment (advertising), $150.00 – 250.00 each.

Plate 697
Tape measures & miscellaneous items including trinket box, $75.00 – 150.00 each.

Plate 698
Tape measures, 1¾" wide, $75.00 – 150.00 each.

Plate 699
Reverse view of Plate 698.

Plate 701
Notebooks (advertising), $50.00 – 75.00 each.

Plate 700
*Notebook, 2½"x4¼", $75.00 –
125.00.*

Plate 702
*Notebook, 2¾"x4¼", $75.00 –
125.00.*

Plate 703
*Notebook, 3½"x2½",
dated 1907, $60.00
– 95.00.*

Plate 704
Notebooks (advertising), $40.00 – 60.00 each.

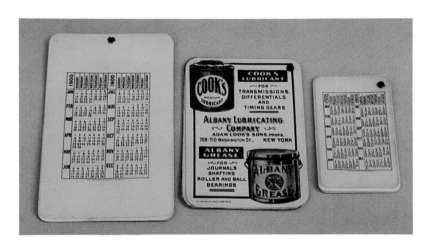

Plate 705
Reverse view of Plate 704.

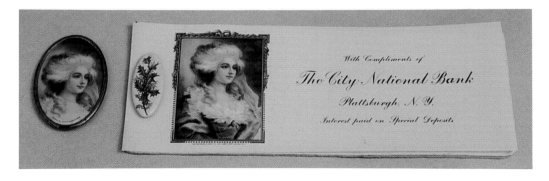

Plate 706
Blotter holder, The Whitehead & Hoag Co. Pat. June 6, 1905 Newark, New Jersey, cover and fastener are celluloid, matching fastener to left, same woman, $75.00 – 125.00.

Plate 707
Notebooks (advertising), 1st notebook copyright 1901, 2nd notebook copyright 1903 The Whitehead & Hoag Co., $50.00 – 75.00 each.

Plate 708
Whisk broom holder, $125.00 – 175.00.

Plate 709
Back view of Plate 708.

Plate 710
Whisk broom holder, 7"x9", $100.00 – 150.00.

Plate 711
Needle case, pat. Feb. 24, 1914, $30.00 – 50.00.

Plate 712
Needle case, $75.00 – 100.00.

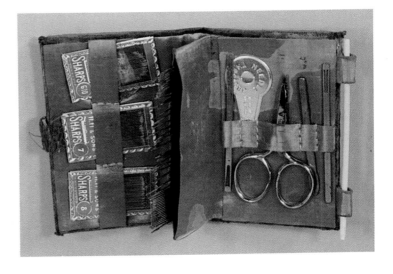

Plate 713
Interior view of Plate 712.

Plate 714
Needle case, 3¾"x3½", $30.00 – 50.00.

Plate 715
Bank, rare, 4½"x3¼", $125.00 – 200.00.

Plate 716
Prayer book, $50.00 – 75.00.

Plate 717
Prayer books, $50.00 – 75.00 each.

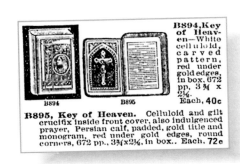

Plate 718
Prayer books, dated 1890 & 1903, $30.00 – 50.00 each.

Plate 719
Prayer book & rosary set, book first published 1865, left purse holds rosary, $125.00 – 175.00 set.

Plate 720
Prayer book, 3¾"x2½", $30.00 – 50.00.

Plate 721
Postcard/photo holder, 8" wide, $150.00 – 225.00.

Plate 722
Pin cushion, 7"x6", $100.00 – 140.00.

Plate 723
Postcard/photo holder, 6½" high, $125.00 – 175.00.

F6248—A s s t d. pink and blue satin finish and transparent red embossed crimped gold edge, hand painted floral and fancy lettering, g o l d traced sides, satin p u ffed lining, 4 brass metal feet. 7x8x3..Each, 36c

F6249—D o u b l e wicker frame, mercerized puffed lined bottom, 2 compartments, ribbon b o w ornament, embossed shaded wild rose celluloid front hand painted and gold traced medallion h e a d center. 2 embossed gilt ornaments, 7½x9x4¾. Each, 71c

Plate 724
Postcard/photo holder, celluloid insert hand painted, 6¼"x2¾"x6¾", $125.00 – 175.00.

Index

Bibliography

Butler Brothers catalogs, 1906 – 1909, 1912, 1915 – 1916.

Doyle, Bernard, W. *Comb Making in America*. Perry Walton, Boston, Mass. 1925.

Fenichell, Stephen. *Plastic, The Making of a Synthetic Century*. Harper Collins Publisher, Inc., New York City, New York, 1996.

Kaufman, M. *The First Century of Plastics*. Plastics Institute, London, 1963.

Mack, Herman, F. *Giant Molecules*. Life Time Inc. New York City, 1966.

Packard, Jerrold, M. *Farewell in Splendor*. Penguin Books, New York City, 1995.

Steele, Gerald, L. *Exploring the World of Plastics*. McKnight Publishing Co., Bloomington, Ill., 1977.

Thompson, Dorothy. *Queen Victoria*. Pantheon Books, New York, 1990.

Wallace, Carol. *Victorian Treasures*. Harry N. Abrams, Inc. New York City, 1973.

Winkler, Gail, Caskey and Moss, Roger, W. *Victorian Interior Decoration*. Henry Holt and Co., New York City, N. Y., 1986.

Woodham – Smith, Cecil. *Queen Victoria*. Alfred A. Knopf, Inc., New York, 1972.

Young, G., M. *Victorian England, Portrait of an Age*. Oxford University Press, London, Oxford, New York City, 1936.

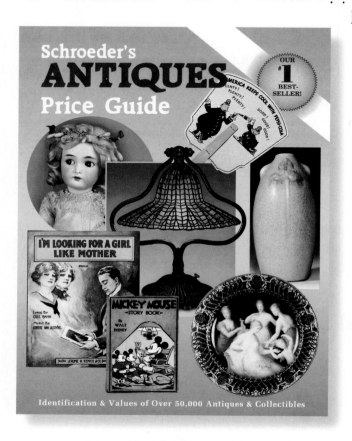